THE
INTP

Personality, Careers, Relationships, &
the Quest for Truth and Meaning

Dr. A.J. Drenth

CONTENTS

INTRODUCTION

INTP is one of sixteen personality types. INTPs love to think and philosophize. They see themselves as questing for truth and meaning. Not only do they seek to know the truth about reality, but to cultivate an abundant and meaningful life. Unfortunately, getting a firm hold on truth and meaning often proves trickier than they anticipate.

Complicating matters further is INTPs' concern for finding and securing their rightful place in the world. This typically involves searching for two things: the right career and the right relationship. Because INTPs envision their optimal career as encapsulating, or at least incorporating, their quest for truth and meaning, it too can prove slippery and elusive.

While often taking a back seat to the INTP's work, relationships can be another point of frustration and difficulty for this type. At times, INTPs may wonder if relationships are even worth their time and effort. Being such independent souls, they may consider whether a romantic partner is really necessary in their quest for happiness.

In light of these challenges, it should not surprise us that INTPs are among the most restless of the personality types. Others may see them as perpetually unsettled, always making and breaking plans. INTPs may also be accused of "thinking too much" or "over-analyzing everything." But such critiques rarely sway or deter them. INTPs know that, regardless of how others perceive them, they must persist in their quest for truth and meaning. Indeed, for the INTP, seeking and exploring is integral to life.

Perhaps the most famous individual associated with the INTP personality type is Albert Einstein. Like other INTPs, Einstein displayed great independence of thought, privileging his own ideas, theories, and projects above all else. He also showed little respect for established conventions and authorities, which he viewed as antagonistic to creativity, individuality, and freedom of thought.

Although I generally agree that Einstein embodied many INTP characteristics, it is equally important to note what he lacked. Namely, he failed to exhibit one of the more common and central features of INTPs—a deep concern for self-knowledge. Indeed, most INTPs see self-knowledge as a critical component of their quest for truth and meaning.

Truth & Meaning in the Modern World

Many INTPs begin their search for truth by looking outside themselves. This is especially common for those reared in extraverted cultures, such as the United States, where they are inundated with messages suggesting that truth and meaning depend on externalities—money, status, relationships, social and religious affiliations, etc. So even though INTPs' natural tendency, as introverts, is to look inward, they may be conditioned by circumstances to first explore what the world has to offer. In this vein, they may scour books on science, religion, philosophy, and the like, hoping to find answers to their questions on truth, meaning, and "how to live."

At this point in history, religion has lost its status as the most tenable and respected authority on objective reality. With increasing evidence for and acceptance of theories like Darwinian evolution and the Big Bang, science has supplanted religion as the leading authority on matters of truth. But as Carl Jung and others have duly noted, science has proven rather ineffective in supplying meaning and purpose to human life. Indeed, the vacuum of existential meaning left in the wake of religion's dethronement is no small problem. Without a viable replacement, many people will be forced to reckon with difficult, even potentially paralyzing, issues such as nihilism and meaninglessness.

In light of this modern situation, INTPs who are unable to successfully resuscitate or reformulate their religious beliefs (assuming they had any to begin with) are forced to look elsewhere for answers to their questions about truth and meaning. Many will turn their sights to psychology, philosophy, or mysticism, all of which speak to the human condition, sans the mythological clothes of traditional religion.

As INTPs proceed to explore and contemplate various perspectives, they discover that "objective" or "absolute" truth is not as easy to identify as they originally imagined. They find there are no quick or easy answers to their questions about truth, meaning, and the human condition. Indeed, just as beauty is "in the eye of the beholder," so it can seem with truth and meaning. As the eminent philosopher, Immanuel Kant, famously professed, "We don't see the world as it is, but as we are."

As INTPs come to see the integral role of human subjectivity in truth and meaning, they increasingly recognize the value and importance of understanding the human mind and psyche, especially their own. Indeed, it is this realization that impelled thinkers such as Nietzsche, Kierkegaard, and others to extol the importance of self-knowledge. These thinkers essentially turned the quest for truth and meaning on its head, removing their gaze from the external world and turning it toward the self, which they saw as the primary source of truth and meaning.

And while Nietzsche and company opened up new vistas for exploring subjective truth and meaning, there remains a fair amount of ambiguity in their thought. One of the main gaps, in my view, involves the question of how one goes about obtaining self-knowledge. What methods and criteria should we use in our attempts to describe and understand ourselves?

Self-Knowledge through Jung's Typology

In his classic work, *Psychological Types*, Carl Jung provides insight into this question of how we might know ourselves. There, he observes that the mind and personality work according to discernable laws and exhibit specific patterns of functioning. Based on his research and clinical observations, as well as his formidable knowledge of history and literature, Jung proffers a theory of personality types (or what he called "psychological types").

One of the beautiful things about Jungian typology is it provides an objective framework for understanding human subjectivity and cultivating self-knowledge. This knowledge can inform and enlighten INTPs' quest for truth and meaning, as well as their search for satisfying work and relationships.

In many cases, INTPs first encounter typology when exploring careers or college majors. After taking various tests and reading pertinent personality descriptions, their interest is piqued. INTPs seem naturally intrigued by the notion of personality types in general and by the features of their own type in particular. This should come as little surprise, as INTPs desperately want to know who they are, how they should live, and the sorts of things they should be doing. Similar to other IN types, INTPs see it necessary to understand themselves—their personality, interests, abilities, and values—before they can act in the world with any degree of confidence or conviction. And because typology promises objective insight into these matters, it can quickly assume a degree of importance for the INTP that extends far beyond its utility in identifying a college major.

As Thinking types, INTPs are inclined to conceive of the self in terms of its structure and utility. In many ways, they see the self as a sort of tool or instrument. In contrast to INFPs, the degree to which the self is unique (or is perceived as unique) is less important to INTPs than is grasping its essential functions and capacities. Hence, for INTPs, the question "Who am I?" might be rephrased as "What kind of tool or instrument am I?" or "What kind of functions am I designed to perform?" By developing a better sense of their psychological structuring and functionality, INTPs feel they can gain insight into how they should conduct or improve their lives.

Ideally, INTPs might envision their lives unfolding in the following way: 1) acquire adequate self-knowledge; 2) apply that self-knowledge to procure a fulfilling work life; 3) find someone to share that life with.

Unfortunately, what often happens is quite the opposite. Before really knowing themselves, they dive into a career, get married, have children, and suddenly find themselves dissatisfied in their careers and relationships. They then feel stuck, seeing it as overly difficult to change or reinvent their careers, or to heal or discontinue their relationships. They therefore live out much of their lives in limbo, feeling restless, aimless, and dissatisfied.

Purpose & Approach

The primary purpose of this book is to help INTPs better understand themselves through the lens of typology. This, in turn, can aid and abet their quest for truth, meaning, and purpose.

This book also strives to help INTPs develop a clearer sense of direction, as well as increased satisfaction, in their work. This is not limited to merely identifying the right career, job, or major. The question of satisfying work is much broader than that and will be explored as such.

Another purpose is to help INTPs understand themselves with respect to relationships, allowing them to develop more meaningful and satisfying partnerships.

The approach of this book is descriptive, theoretical, and to some degree, prescriptive. Descriptively, it details the interests, characteristics, and psychology of INTPs. This includes descriptions of how INTPs think, behave, and engage (or fail to engage) with others. It also tackles some of INTPs' biggest concerns, such as their quest for truth and meaning in life.

To help us understand the structure and origins of the INTP's thoughts and behavior, we will draw on the theoretics of Jung, Myers and Briggs, as well as the work of my colleague Elaine Schallock and myself. This includes exploring the INTP's functions and the dynamical interactions of those functions in the INTP's "functional stack." We will devote particular attention to the relationship between INTPs' dominant function, Introverted Thinking (Ti), and their inferior function, Extraverted Feeling (Fe), a tension that has been overlooked or severely underestimated in other works.

With regard to prescription, part of my interest in typology involves the degree to which our understanding of the structure and functioning of each personality type lends itself to prescriptions for individuation and personal growth. In other words, to what degree does the "is" of a type inform the "ought?" I am inclined to believe that typology offers significant insight into how each personality type might function to maximize its growth and well-being.

At this point, I also wish to disclose my own status as an INTP. I realize this may be viewed as an advantage or disadvantage with respect to the value and credibility of this book. The disadvantage, of course, is that my understanding of the INTP might be skewed by my personal biases and experiences. The advantage is that I have not only had the opportunity to study INTPs from without, but also to live and experience life as an INTP from within. And while many Personality Junkie readers might attest to the value of my conjectures, I invite you, the reader, to be your own judge.

Overview

In Chapter 1, I provide a general overview, as well as a function-by-function analysis, of the INTP personality type, including a look at the tug-of-war between the INTP's dominant (Ti) and inferior (Fe) function. We will explore at length the various manifestations of INTPs' inferior Fe, a function whose profound effects are too often overlooked or underestimated.

In Chapter 2, we will explore INTPs' typical course of growth and development across the lifespan. We will frame our discussion in terms of three phases of development, granting particular attention to Phase II, which extends from late childhood through midlife. In Phase II, INTPs encounter the most pressing challenges with regard to their career, relationships, and identity. It is also the time in which they struggle most with the opposing desires and interests of their Ti and Fe. By understanding the potential traps and pitfalls of Phase II, INTPs are more likely to avoid having to learn life's lessons "the hard way."

Chapter 3 explores what I call the "negative potentials" of the INTP personality type. This includes a careful look at the INTP's "dark side," as well as the degree to which INTPs are prone to various psychological problems such as depression, ADD, autism/Asperger's, narcissism, and schizoid/schizotypal personality disorders.

Chapter 4 tackles one of the INTP's most poignant and recurrent concerns—their quest for truth and meaning. In the first half of the chapter, we will explore INTPs' struggle to find consistent sources or landmarks of meaning, as well as their fears and concerns about meaninglessness. We will also consider the role of their inferior function in fueling their quest for meaning and their meaning-related fears. The second half of this chapter focuses on INTPs' search for convergent truth. This will include an assessment of the effects of this quest on their psychological well-being, as well as what a healthy approach to truth-seeking might look like for INTPs.

Chapter 5 explores some of INTPs' political, religious, and philosophical propensities. This will include analyses of the relative contributions of each of the INTP's four functions to the ways in which they see and understand the world.

The importance of satisfying work for INTPs cannot be overstated. Unfortunately, INTPs encounter numerous roadblocks in their quest for a fulfilling career. In Chapter 6, we will dive deep into some of their most pressing career concerns. This includes addressing issues such as the degree to which they should focus on the intrinsic versus extrinsic value of their work, the pluses and minuses of working independently, the potential merits of a day job, creative versus analytical careers, etc. We will also consider some of the INTP's most common career strengths and interests areas, drawing on the six "RIASEC" interest themes—Realistic, Investigative, Artistic, Social, Enterprising, and Conventional—developed by John Holland. This will include analyses of how the INTPs' functions link up with their top interest areas. We will also examine the relative merits of specific careers and majors—the hard sciences, social/moral sciences, computers/IT, freelancing, scholarship, medicine, psychology, etc.— in light of the INTP's personality, skills, values, and interests.

Chapter 7 explores the ways INTPs think and function with respect to relationships. Because of the polarized nature of their Ti and Fe functions, INTPs often display a sort of love-hate attitude toward relationships. On the one hand, they cherish their autonomy and independence (Ti), while on the other, they seek love and companionship (Fe). As we will see, the way in which INTPs deal with relationships is in many ways reflective of the way they deal with the inherent challenges of their own personality type. This chapter starts out by exploring the question of whether INTPs need or should pursue relationships at all. In doing so, it provides an inside look into the way INTPs think about and approach relationships, as well as their unconscious motivations. In the remainder of the chapter, we explore the following issues: relationships as a forum for learning and experimentation, the value of implementing an "openness & honest policy," the danger of concealing negative thoughts and assumptions, INTP communication issues, Ti-Fe identity issues (i.e.,"Lone Wolf" versus "Mr. Nice Guy"), and INTP attitudes toward family and parenting.

Chapter 8 might be viewed as an extension of Chapter 7. It explores, on a type-by-type basis, how INTPs may fare when paired with various personality types. We will devote most our time to examining their compatibility with Intuitive personality types, types who are most likely to comprise a suitable "mindmate" for the INTP.

Chapter 9 compares and contrasts INTPs with related personality types—INTJs, ENTPs, ISTPs, and INFPs. By highlighting noteworthy similarities and differences, this chapter will help INTPs better distinguish themselves from these other types.

1. PROFILE AND FUNCTIONS

INTPs comprise roughly 3-4% of the general population. As is commonly the case among Thinking types, there appears to be at least twice as many INTP males as females.

INTPs use Introverted Thinking (Ti) as their dominant function. As we will later discuss in greater detail, Ti can be associated with independence and intensity of thought. While Ti may compel INTPs to focus on a relatively narrow range of interests, their auxiliary function, Extraverted Intuition (Ne), searches for broad connections across various subjects and knowledge areas. INTPs commonly explore topics like philosophy, science, religion, history, psychology, and evolutionary theory. By surveying a breadth of knowledge domains, they develop a clearer view of the "big picture," of how everything fits together.

In addition to their concern for apprehending the big picture, INTPs are also interested in discerning the fundamental nature of things. This can be understood in terms of their Ti's tendency toward reductionism, to boiling everything down to its bare essentials. In searching for what we might call the "foundations of everything," INTPs commonly wrestle with physical, as well as metaphysical, concepts and theories. Their Ne's penchant for the big picture, combined with their Ti's concern for essentials, explains why INTPs are often well-described as philosophers.

But INTPs are not merely essentialist philosophers. They are also existentialists, concerned with questions of existence and "how to live." They are not only concerned with truth, but also with meaning. Indeed, if we were to liken INTPs to a coin, we might put truth on one side and meaning on the other. Acutely aware of the brevity of life, INTPs strive to ensure that their lives and work are as authentic and meaningful as possible.

The INTP from Without

When vacationing from their personal projects and investigations, INTPs can be quirky, witty, and engaging. Since they extravert both Feeling (Fe) and Intuition (Ne), they can have a certain charm, approachability, and congeniality about them. Einstein aptly embodied such traits.

Furthermore, when discussing topics that interest them, INTPs can be stimulating conversationalists. Their ever-active minds quickly connect one topic to another, paving the way for broad-ranging dialogues. If disinterested however, such as when forced to endure protracted small talk, INTPs will quickly zone out or find a way to redirect the conversation. Despite appearing outwardly personable, INTPs are more interested in discussing ideas than they are the commonplace details of people's lives. They enjoy analyzing what makes people tick—their motivations, interests, patterns, and propensities. This allows INTPs to further hone and refine their theories (Ti-Ne) of human nature (Fe).

Like other introverts, INTPs can be anxious and self-conscious characters. It is not uncommon for them to display a handful of nervous habits, or at least some indication they are not fully at ease. They often avoid direct eye contact, as though the gaze of their interlocutor may somehow harm them or render them incapable of thinking or communicating. INTPs may also feel insecure about the scattered nature of their Ne expressions, which may at times sound more like disjointed ramblings than erudite expositions. Feeling that someone else is closely watching or critiquing their expressions only furthers their sense of insecurity.

INTPs can also be rather slow in disclosing the true contents of their inner world. As strange as it may seem to some, INTPs conceal some of their most dominant personality features, namely, their cerebral, rational side. Indeed, it may only be a select few who are granted full access to this side of the INTP. Perhaps the best way of sampling INTPs' inner world is through their work, such as by reading something they have written. This may explain why INTPs often take interest in writing, which provides a forum for more robust and precise self-expression.

In light of their reluctance to freely reveal the rational side of their personality, as well as the scattered nature of their Ne expressions, INTPs feel their true level of knowledge and competence is often lost on others. This is especially common in the workplace, where their lack of enthusiasm for organizational life, combined with their quirky outward demeanor, may be mistaken for incompetence.

INTP Gender Differences

While we won't go too far out of our way to tease out INTP gender differences, a 2001 research paper entitled, "Gender Differences in Personality Traits Across Cultures," found surprisingly consistent gender differences across 26 cultures (Costa, et al.). Specifically, the researchers found that "women tend to be higher in negative affect, submissiveness, and nurturance and more concerned with feelings than ideas." Men, by contrast, tested higher in assertiveness, excitement seeking, and a preference for ideas over feelings. Since many of these findings seem to fall along Thinking-Feeling lines, it does not seem unreasonable to suggest that female INTPs may, to some extent, have more in common with Feeling types than male INTPs do. They may, for instance, display stronger nurturing propensities.

More recent research (2013) from the University of Pennsylvania indicates that female brains display greater neuronal connectivity *between* hemispheres, whereas males exhibit more connections *within* each hemisphere. The researchers suggested that, according to these findings, females are more likely to integrate right (e.g., intuitive, emotional) and left-brained (analytical) styles in their processing, whereas males will tend to show less integration. If we apply these findings to INTPs, male INTPs may exhibit a greater disconnect between their Thinking and Feeling, creating an even larger gulf between their dominant Ti and inferior Fe functions. If this is the case, it would further support the notion that INTP females are apt to be somewhat more "F-like" than INTP males.

The Functional Stack

Each personality type is thought to use four main functions that comprise its "functional stack." The functions in the functional stack are ordered according to their degree of strength and differentiation, as well as their availability for conscious employment. The most differentiated and conscious function is appropriately dubbed the "dominant function," which is followed by the auxiliary, tertiary, and inferior functions respectively.

The dominant function represents the core strength and defining characteristic of each type. When engrossed in an activity that fully engages the dominant function, we tend to feel alert and alive, doing what we were "born to do." The auxiliary function, which can also be well-developed and useful, might be viewed as the co-pilot or sidekick to the dominant.

Falling toward the bottom of the functional stack, the tertiary and inferior are significantly less conscious and developed than the top two functions. Despite being less conscious, however, these functions, particularly the inferior function, can play a prominent role in the personality.

Dominant Function: "The Captain." The signature strength of the personality type.

Auxiliary Function: "The Helpful Sidekick." The chief assistant to the dominant function.

Tertiary Function: "The Adolescent." Relatively unconscious and undifferentiated.

Inferior Function: "The Child." The least differentiated and conscious of the four functions.

The INTP's functional stack:

Dominant: Introverted Thinking (Ti)

Auxiliary: Extraverted Intuition (Ne)

Tertiary: Introverted Sensing (Si)

Inferior: Extraverted Feeling (Fe)

We will now take a closer look at each of these functions.

Dominant Function: Introverted Thinking (Ti)

In order to understand INTPs, or other IP types, we must first recognize the full implications of their dominant function (Ti) being a Judging function. Namely, since Ti is a Judging function, INTPs are predominantly inner Judgers. So rather than remaining in a state of openness, INTPs, like EJ types (whose Judging function is also dominant), are compelled to seek closure and have things settled in their minds. They want to hammer down what they believe in order to have a platform from which to make important decisions about their lives. When their beliefs are shaken into state of uncertainty, they can feel anxious, unsettled, and aimless.

INTPs can also resemble EJs in their tendency to think in terms of what they should be doing. They like to set goals and objectives for themselves, approaching life with a sense of intentionality. At least when it comes to initiating tasks, they can be as disciplined as any EJ type. It is mainly after initiating a task that INTPs get sidetracked and start looking more like EPs. This is understandable in light of the ordering of their functional stack. They start off with a judgment (Ti), which impels them to begin work on a task. Once initiated, however, their next function is a Perceiving function (Ne), which can cause them to get distracted or sidetracked, even to the point of losing sight of their original purpose. This can be frustrating for INTPs, since the endpoint or "goal" of their functional stack (i.e., their inferior function) involves reaching a state of judgment or closure (Fe). This may also partly explain why they can at times be careless or sloppy in their work, since their drive to finish a project may override their desire for precision or accuracy.

What is tricky about INTPs' inner Judging process is their judgments typically remain concealed from others. While Extraverts and Judging types are quicker to express their thoughts, INTPs are inclined to sit on their judgments before sharing them. In fact, the vast majority of INTPs' judgments go unsaid, leaving others with little clue as to what they are thinking.

In being slow to express their judgments, INTPs are often viewed as good and patient listeners. But as inner Judgers, they are neither as patient, nor as eager to listen, as they might outwardly appear. Nor are they as passive or relaxed as their appearance might suggest, since their Ti contributes an inner seriousness and intentionality that prompts them to pursue their own agenda.

Because INTPs like to work independently and uninterruptedly, they can get frustrated when others interrupt or make demands of them. This is especially true when their thoughts are flowing and they don't want to lose their momentum. In such instances, INTPs may think (although will rarely ever say) something along these lines: "I wish people would just leave me alone so I can get on with my work."

One of the most important things to understand about INTPs is their sense that the one and only thing in the world they can control is themselves. Since their outer Judging function (Fe) is in the inferior position, they feel uncomfortable making judgments or decisions about external situations, especially when there is a potential for introducing conflict. This is why they become frustrated, even resentful, when the world makes demands of them. Such demands disrupt their self-directed Ti process and force them to attend to externalities they feel less interested in or capable of controlling.

This prompts the question of how INTPs should respond to such "intrusions." Should they abandon their inner Ti process and shift into extraverted Perceiving (Ne) to assess the situation? Or should they resist the intrusion by mustering some measure of Fe judgment? Since the latter option requires more energy and gumption for INTPs, the former is their default approach, which, as we've seen, leads others to see them as receptive and adaptable. But again, this is sort of an illusion, since their preferred mode of operation is Ti rather than Ne. I therefore suggest that INTPs are really not spontaneous in the way that EP types are. INTPs may be spontaneous (or impulsive) when they are at the helms, but when it comes to spontaneously responding to the outside world, they tend to drag their heels.

Yep!

What is Introverted Thinking (Ti)?

Having now considered the implications of INTPs' Ti as a dominant Judging function, we will now expound on the nature of Ti itself.

Ti involves the application of logic and reason for the sake of understanding a given situation, system, or problem. INTPs use Ti to bring structure, order, and clarity to their thoughts and inner world. They also use Ti to direct and order their lives and projects, including setting personal goals and objectives. Consequently, Ti can be associated with independence, self-discipline, and self-regulation.

Immanuel Kant is a great example of a highly self-disciplined and self-regulated INTP. Kant is notorious for never having traveled outside his town. He developed a routine—arising each day at the same time, writing through the morning, dining with friends at lunch, taking a walk in the afternoon, and studying and reading in the evening—that he followed with great consistency. Indeed, one could argue that his degree of self-regimentation was instrumental to his profound philosophical achievements.

As suggested from its introverted direction, Ti is directed toward the self and its ideas. In this sense, it stands in contradistinction to Te, which strives to make external systems more rational. Like Kant, INTPs work to ensure that their lives, worldview, and personal philosophy are orderly and rational. Their Ti compels them to constantly establish and reestablish inner order. INTJs, by contrast, whose dominant function is Intuition (Ni), are far less concerned about consciously maintaining inner order.

Ti is less interested in working with facts than it is with concepts and ideas. Jung writes: "His [sic] ideas have their origin not in objective data, but in his subjective foundation." INTPs are constantly digging into the background of their own thoughts in order to better understand their origins and to ensure their thinking is founded on a solid conceptual platform.

Generally speaking, Ti (along with Ne) finds it easier to identify inconsistencies or logical shortcomings—to assert what is *not* true—than to identify and confidently assert what *is* true. INTPs can quickly locate inconsistencies or logical shortcomings in a given theory or argument. They excel in pinpointing exceptions or imagining scenarios in which a proposed explanation might breakdown. Due to their acute sensitivity to theoretical exceptions, they can be quick

Negative nancy

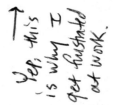

Yep, this is why I get frustrated at work.

(sometimes too quick) to discard entire theories, throwing out the proverbial baby with the bathwater.

INTJs, by contrast, seem less deterred by ostensible exceptions (especially those pertaining to their own theories), perhaps believing they will eventually be explained or rectified. Since INTJs are predominantly perceptive and their Ni works convergently, they tend to be a bit more cautious and careful on the front end, but after reaching a conclusion, they are less apt to vacillate or change their minds.

When INTPs' Ti and Ne are functioning constructively or synthetically (as opposed to critically), they can be seen as employing a sort of trial-and-error approach to theory-making. They start out with a given (Ti) and then use their auxiliary Ne to explore various connections and possibilities. This again contrasts with the INTJ's mode of operation. INTJs display more patience on the front end, allowing the theory to intuitively emerge in its entirety (Ni), and then carefully analyze and enumerate it via Te.

yep

The Ti-Ne duo is an interesting one. As we will discuss in our next section, Ne functions divergently and exponentially increases the number of options and possibilities. Ti, by contrast, as an introverted function, is more reductionistic in nature. Instead of moving forward and multiplying ideas, it works backwards, paring things down to their bare essentials. In this sense, Ti can resemble Ni, which works more convergently and reductively than Ne.

INTP theorists and writers are likely aware of the tension between their Ti and Ne, even if they don't describe it in such terms. When Ti takes hold, they become more focused on clarifying basic ideas and concepts. They may even construct charts and diagrams in hopes of maximizing the coherency, consistency, and structure of their ideas. While at times helpful, when this hardcore front-end structuring fails to produce the clean and cogent framework they desire, they tend to swing back toward the less predictable methods of Ne. This might, for instance, involve doing more writing and less categorizing, trusting that connections and insights will emerge through the less conscious creative process.

In my experience, INTPs are typically happiest when functioning somewhere between Ti and Ne, rather than toward either extreme. Most often, the understanding or expression they are seeking emerges with the aid of Ne, rather than through strict use of Ti. Hence, writing (as well as other creative arts) can serve as helpful tools of discovery for INTPs. Rarely can INTPs know in advance what will emerge from the creative act, which is one reason creative work is so interesting and enjoyable for them. INTJs, by contrast, often describe the writing process as more burdensome or draining. This may be partly due to the fact that INTJs seem to have a better sense of where they are headed than INTPs do, making the writing process seem more like work and less like discovery.

Auxiliary Function: Extraverted Intuition (Ne)

INTPs use Extraverted Intuition (Ne) as their auxiliary function. Because Ne is their first extraverted function, it is their primary tool for engaging with the outside world and communicating with others.

In its verbal incarnation, Ne resembles a sort of "brainstorming aloud." Consequently, INTPs' speech is often sporadic and uneven, sometimes rambling, as their Ne randomly bounces from one idea to the next. Listeners may struggle to discern exactly what the INTP is trying to say, as one idea begets associations with countless others. To get a sense of what this is like, imagine an idea placed in the center of five other ideas, all of which seem connected in a meaningful way. This associative propensity of Ne can make it difficult for INTPs (or other NP types) to cogently express themselves in a streamlined fashion. They may struggle to narrow all the verbal and ideational possibilities into a single linear expression. Even ideas that seem inwardly logical and sensible to INTPs may become muddled or incoherent when conveyed through Ne. This is why INTPs often feel more confident expressing themselves in writing, which affords them more time to arrange their ideas in a logical fashion. It is also why INTPs prefer the role of interviewer or facilitator over that of the interviewee or lecturer. Ne seems more conducive to responding in short bursts than to generating lengthy monologues.

In its receptive role, Ne prompts INTPs to gather information. Unlike Extraverted Sensing (Se), Ne is not attuned to concrete, sense data. Indeed, INTPs are among the oblivious to environmental details of all types, commonly missing things that seem obvious to others. Ne looks beyond sense data, allowing INTPs to discern unseen patterns, possibilities, and potentials. It is constantly scanning for relationships or patterns within pools of facts, ideas, or experiences. INTPs commonly exercise this receptive element of Ne in activities such as reading, researching, listening to talk radio, or engaging in conversation.

Ne also confers an ample measure of open-mindedness. Unlike Ni, which works convergently and comes with a sense of conviction, Ne works divergently and is less apt to commit to a single conclusion (at least not for very long). Ne sees multiple explanations and possibilities for nearly everything ("The possibilities are endless!"). This can make it difficult for INTPs to be consistent in their judgments and decisions, since they often end up second-guessing themselves. While their Ti pushes for closure, Ne counters by rallying for more options and alternatives. In many cases, Ne wins out, interjecting just enough new or contradictory information to keep INTPs in a state of indecision. Indeed, it is not uncommon for INTPs to feel entirely confident one day, only to feel ambivalent and uncertain the next.

Relatedly, Ne sees many matters as grey or ambiguous. INTPs typically see truth on both sides of an issue, which can prevent them from latching onto unwarranted judgments or premature conclusions. This is why they are often perceived as fair and even-handed arbiters.

Ne also contributes an openness to alternative lifestyles. It would not be unusual, for instance, for INTPs to experiment with vegetarianism, consider joining a commune, go a week or two without showering, or decide they are going to try living out of a van.

Ne can also engender a sense of adventure, expectancy, and wonderment toward life's mysteries and contingencies. It confers a sense of blind anticipation, of not knowing who or what will manifest next on one's life journey. In this sense Ne can have a mystical or spiritual flavor, involving an openness or curiosity toward life's contingencies. The experience of "synchronicity"—roughly defined as a sense of meaningful coincidence—is not uncommon among INTPs who are open to what we might call Ne spirituality. Both Kant and Einstein reported a strong sense of awe and wonder in their contemplations of the cosmos.

On the more negative side of things, Ne may contribute to a persistent sense of restlessness or dissatisfaction. INTPs may find themselves wanting to break out of certain situations or circumstances in order to experience more novelty, freedom, and autonomy. They might feel compelled to quit their job or break off a relationship in hopes of discovering something more stimulating. This is not without its social consequences, however, as those who consistently act on such promptings may be perceived as fickle, irresponsible, or erratic.

Like other NPs, INTPs often have a love-hate relationship with their Ne. They love the fact that it keeps them open-minded in their ideation and lifestyle, while at times fatiguing of their perpetual state of restlessness or vacillation. Indeed, it can seem that at the very moment INTPs are feeling good about a theory or decision, their Ne steps in and shakes things up. This has obvious implications for INTPs who are trying to make important decisions about their careers or relationships. It can leave them feeling discouraged and restless, worried that they may never find what they are looking for or produce anything of lasting value. Since Ne can be a sort of hit or miss function, INTPs often require a great deal of time and experimentation to approach a higher level of confidence and certainty.

(handwritten annotation: "Time Experimentation")

Tertiary Function: Introverted Sensing (Si)

Unlike Ne, INTPs' tertiary function, Introverted Sensing (Si), is a conservative and convergent function. It engenders attachments to past experiences and past precedent—to the routine, familiar, and predictable.

Types with Si in their functional stack, including INTPs, tend to eat a fairly routine or consistent diet, "eating to live" rather than "living to eat." They are also conservative with regard to their resources, tending toward saving over spending. Minimalists to the core, INTPs have a diminished need for novel physical pleasures and material comforts. Their mates may get frustrated with their tendency to shoot down proposed expenditures, most of which seem superfluous or otherwise unnecessary to the bare bones pragmatist that is the INTP.

It is important to recognize that Si manifests somewhat differently depending on its position in the functional stack. For types using Si as the dominant or auxiliary function (SJ types), it contributes an adherence to existing facts, traditions, worldviews, or methods. SJs are typically less equipped to spawn new ideas of lasting worth, since this requires stronger powers of Ne. Therefore, SJs tend to align their beliefs and behaviors with an existing standard or tradition, granting them a sense of consistency and security.

When Si falls lower in the functional stack, as is the case for INTPs, it fails to deliver the strength of conviction commonly seen in SJ types. It also deemphasizes traditional beliefs and instead relies on INTPs' past experiences and synthesized knowledge. INTPs use their Si recall as a sort of check and balance for their Ti-Ne ideas. In time, INTPs may experience a heightened sense of Si conviction, a sense that they are slowly progressing toward what they are seeking.

Si can also help INTPs develop effective habits, as we saw in the case of Kant. As INTPs observe themselves over time, they can identify behaviors that allow them to function most optimally and to feel most satisfied. Then, when they start to get off track, their Si can step in and remind them of those behaviors, aiding their return to a more balanced and healthy state. In combination with Ti, Si helps them hone and perfect their method of living.

A commonly overlooked role of Si is its perception of internal bodily sensations—the body as felt and experienced from within. Perhaps more than any other function, it provides access to the raw and basic sense of "being" that exists apart from thought or outward stimuli. Historically, Eastern philosophical and religious traditions have done a much better job exploring and cultivating this dimension than those of the West. This feature of Si is brought to the fore during activities that require close attention to one's internal bodily state. This includes practices like yoga, Tai-Chi, Feldenkrais, meditation, and various relaxation techniques.

INTPs interested in exploring this element of Si may find great delight and derive much benefit from these sorts of practices, which are especially useful in developing the bodily awareness necessary to relax, focus, and mitigate anxiety. They can therefore aid INTPs in their intellectual and creative work. Such practices can also be interesting and meaningful in their own right, persuading INTPs to take a break from their usual Ti mode in order to relax, perceive, and explore the wonderland of their inner body.

Inferior Function: Extraverted Feeling (Fe)

The inferior function represents the ultimate goal or attractor point for each personality type's growth and development. It motivates and draws us forward, compelling us to move toward greater wholeness. It promises a new mode of existence, one that is wholly different from that of the dominant function, which is why it is often experienced and described as "magical."

The inferior function opposes the dominant and in many ways has its own agenda. It can cause us to act in ways that are grossly inconsistent with our type's typical presentation. While it is possible for the inferior to be integrated in a healthy fashion, this is often not the case. More typically, the inferior manifests in extreme ways, like a child demanding attention. In such instances, we abandon the values and objectives our dominant function in order to indulge, gratify, or placate the inferior.

The inferior can play a prominent role in obsessive, compulsive, or addictive behaviors. "In the grip" of our inferior function, we feel locked into a certain mood, attitude, or behavior, one we cannot easily escape. We become narrow-minded, irrational, impetuous, self-indulgent, and lose our sense of humor. In many ways, religious notions, such as sin and the devil, seem closely related to grip experiences with the inferior function.

When a given function is in the inferior position, rather than the dominant or auxiliary position, it tends to be more sensitive and touchy. Those who know how to "push our buttons" have usually discovered a way to offend, irritate, or threaten our inferior function. And since the inferior is rather unconscious and undeveloped, it often responds in an all-or-nothing, childish fashion. The sort of childish behavior associated with the inferior function is closely related to what are sometimes described as "ego issues" (e.g., ego hypersensitivity, ego defensiveness, grandiosity, etc.).

As is true of other types, INTPs are often blinded to the degree to which their inferior function, Extraverted Feeling (Fe), impacts their decisions and behavior. In order to avoid being subconsciously controlled and unduly influenced by their Fe, INTPs can benefit from understanding Fe in general, as well as the ways it tends to manifest in their own personality type.

Interesant

What Is Extraverted Feeling?

The Feeling function weighs and evaluates our affective responses to the world. Since it is rather unconscious and undifferentiated in Thinking types, Thinkers are often unaware of their own emotions and Feeling judgments. Feeling types, by contrast, are not only aware of their emotions in general, but are also attuned to emotional nuance and subtleties (just as Thinkers are more attuned to logical subtleties). Indeed, for every emotion in a Thinking type's arsenal, a Feeler may distinguish numerous feelings or feeling tones. Because Feelers discern a greater breadth of emotional variations and nuances, they may feel that words are inadequate to capture and convey their experiences, prompting many to turn to poetry, music, and the arts as alternative forms of self-expression.

The Feeling function also pertains to the development of tastes. Tastes are qualitative preferences—likes and dislikes. This is another reason Feeling types are drawn to the arts, which provide a forum for developing and refining their tastes.

Extraverted Feeling (Fe) is an extraverted Judging function. While the extraverted Perceiving functions (e.g., Ne) express things in an open-ended fashion (e.g., "What do you think about…?"), the extraverted Judging functions utilize declarative statements (e.g., "I feel that…" or "I don't like…"). Such differences are also conveyed in expressional tone. When J-types (especially EJs) ask questions, their tone may seem insincere, since an attitude of outer receptiveness does not come naturally to them. Similarly, P-types (especially IPs), may at times appear awkward or uncomfortable making firm declarative statements.

While the content of an Fe expression need not be highly emotional, there is a discernable difference in its packaging compared to that of Extraverted Thinking (Te). Te presents as rather dry, lifeless, and monotonal. It can seem flat in its tone, volume, and inflection, especially in TJ types. This is because Te is unconcerned with connecting with others on an emotional plane. Its purpose is to convey information in a literal and explicit fashion. This can make it difficult to read the underlying emotions of TJ types.

When Fe types (especially FJs) engage with others, they are looking to create a shared bond of feeling. They want their feelings to be understood and reciprocated in a way that allows both parties to get on the same emotional page.

Fe is sometimes described as more "superficial" than Introverted Feeling (Fi). This is partly because, as an extraverted function, Fe tends to work broadly and extensively rather than deeply and intensively. This ostensible superficiality is most clearly exemplified in TP types. TP politicians, for example, can appear extremely sincere and affable (Fe), while furtively harboring an alternative Ti agenda. Such individuals may use their Fe in deceptive and disingenuous ways, using it to ingratiate themselves to others in order to advance their hidden agendas.

Harmony vs. Helping

Since Fe is INTPs' inferior function, it is often more sensitive and less resilient than it is in FJ types. This can make INTPs extremely uncomfortable in emotional situations, especially those involving potential conflict or disharmony.

Because of their Fe's concern for maintaining external harmony (or what may be better understood as its discomfort with disharmony), INTPs may abstain from expressing their judgments in order to avoid unsettling others. While not as overtly warm or effusive as FJ types, INTPs can be sensitive to others' feelings and may go out of their way to avoid hurting or offending them. For instance, in the midst of a discussion, an INTP may want to explain how human mating practices are primarily a product of evolutionary pressures. But if she suspects that others may take offense to such an explanation, she may withhold it to avoid introducing disharmony.

Although functioning as superficial peacemakers, INTPs are generally slower to go out of their way to help others (at least in direct, hands-on ways). Especially early in their development, most forgo community service and avoid investing extensive time and energy helping others. This is particularly evident when under stress. If burdened by too many external pressures or demands, INTPs' willingness to help others is one of the first things to go.

[margin: Absolutely]

[margin: Yep — at work]

In short, INTPs' Fe is more concerned with preserving harmony than it is with extensive helping. This is especially true early in life, when they have yet to achieve their Ti goals. Once those goals have been satisfactorily met, however, they may become more benevolent. We can see this with Einstein, for instance, who displayed increasing beneficence and generosity toward people in the second half of his life.

Reluctance to Extravert Judgment

Unlike J-types, INTPs are uncomfortable issuing orders and directives. This is why, whenever possible, they shy away from leadership roles. For the same reason, parenting and disciplining children can be challenging for INTPs.

[margin: yep, parenting]

We've already discussed one reason why INTPs are slow to extravert judgment—their fear of disharmony. But there are other reasons as well. One is that Ne is the first extraverted function in their functional stack. So instead of directly expressing a judgment, they may do so in less direct ways, such as through hints or questions (e.g., "Are you sure you want to do that?").

They may also refrain from expressing judgments because they have yet to settle an issue in their own minds. INTPs never want to be seen as dogmatic, closed-minded, or unnuanced in their thinking.

[margin: Absolutely!]

Relatedly, they are naturally slow to advise others, especially with regard to F-related matters. This is because INTPs don't want to get it wrong, to deal with the aftermath of being wrong, or to make decisions that involve or affect other people.

As will be discussed in our relationships chapter, INTPs may also forgo extraverting judgment for fear of saying something that will irreparably damage their relationship or their partner's perception of them. They may work hard to uphold their self-perception of being nice and considerate (Fe), even if this belies the more independent and self-focused nature of their Ti.

Because of their reluctance to or difficulty in extraverting judgment, INTPs may at times act tyrannically, making sudden executive decisions without any prior communication. In such instances, others may feel incredulous as to why the INTP failed to discuss the issue with them first. Moreover, after restraining their feelings for some time, INTPs may display sudden outbursts of anger and frustration. They may also resort to more passive-aggressive forms of resistance, such as intentionally staying late at the office to protest their domestic dissatisfaction.

In short, having an inferior Fe can hinder INTPs ability to communicate directly and effectively with others. It can take a great deal of courage, practice, and trust for INTPs to assert themselves a la Fe, particularly when discussing controversial, relational, or otherwise uncomfortable issues.

Desire to Teach/Enlighten Others

INTPs strive to discover knowledge or wisdom they can use to enlighten the world. Like FJs, they like the idea of enlightening others regarding how they might live better lives (Fe). But as we've seen, INTPs can struggle when it comes to directly expressing their judgments. They are more comfortable exchanging ideas by way of their auxiliary

Ne than delivering direct Fe advice. INTPs can also become impatient with those who are slow to understand or embrace their ideas. They often expect others to learn as quickly and independently as they do. Therefore, INTPs tend to have mixed feelings when it comes to teaching or counseling others.

Desire for Affirmation/Validation

As we've seen, Fe seeks to establish shared connections of feeling with others. When a successful connection occurs, it produces a sense of validation, of being valued and understood. While most INTPs can do a fair job at reading others' emotions and discerning the appropriate social response, they often fail to "feel" what others are feeling. In other words, they experience *cognitive* rather than *affective* empathy.

(Interesting, tell me more)

Despite their difficulty in connecting with others on a feeling level, INTPs' Fe still desires the same sense of affirmation and validation that FJs experience when engaging with people. This desire for affirmation can be seen as a motivating force behind INTPs' quest for recognition and achievement. It also explains why many INTPs score high as Enneagram Threes (3) and display certain narcissistic tendencies.

Since INTPs rely on others for affirmation, they often feel they cannot live without at least one other person in their lives. Their fear of being alone or unneeded may play a significant role in their perceived need for romantic relationships. There are also times, however, when INTPs feel incredibly independent (Ti) and may even convince themselves they don't need other people. This is especially true in periods where they are completely absorbed in the creative flow of their work. But after long droughts of human interaction, INTPs begin to feel that something is missing from their lives. This prompts them to reinitiate contact with others, at least until they feel compelled to assert their independence again.

my entire life!!

Childlike & Slippery Emotions

For most INTPs, their Fe is rather naive and childlike. They may be easily moved by cheesy romantic comedies or sappy love songs, anything that unconsciously incites their Fe emotions. Their emotional naiveté can make them easy targets for love-at-first-sight sorts of infatuation. They are particularly susceptible to seduction by extraverted Feeling types, whose Fe warmth can bypass INTPs' typical channels of logic and appeal directly to their less conscious Fe.

As is typically the case with the inferior function, there is an all-or-nothing character to INTPs' Fe. Their emotions seem to have a mind of their own, coming and going as they please. Consequently, INTPs feel awkward and inept in emotional situations, since they often fail to experience the situationally-appropriate emotions. As we've seen, INTPs usually know which emotions are appropriate, but without experiencing them directly, they can be clumsy or mechanical in emotional situations.

In many cases, INTPs experience emotions at inopportune times. They may, for instance, experience feelings of love and affection when apart from their partners, but may struggle to contact those feelings, let alone effectively communicate them, while together.

Although INTPs may struggle to directly contact their own emotions, they can be adept at overriding or detaching from them, even functioning as though they didn't exist. Therefore, they may not struggle with the same measure of pain, guilt, regret, or shame as other types. Indeed, others may be surprised how quickly INTPs can seemingly resume "business as usual" after what most would consider tragic or traumatic circumstances.

Hypersensitivity & Anger toward Lack of Fe Control

Since Fe is more conscious and developed in FJ types, it is capable of stepping in, taking charge, and managing others' behavior. While FJs (especially EFJs) are confident in their ability to control the outside world, their poorly developed Ti may confer little in the way of inner control. We see the opposite phenomenon in INTPs, who experience a strong sense of inner control, but feel largely inept with regard to their ability to control others.

To deal with this Fe deficit, one of the INTP's primary strategies is to avoid situations that make Fe demands of them. This may, for instance, involve eschewing positions of leadership or minimizing interpersonal contacts. INTPs feel it safer and easier to be responsible only for themselves.

Unfortunately, life rarely allows INTPs to remain in a state of Ti utopia for long. At some point, they must poke their head out of their shell and engage with people. And where there are people, there are bound to be Fe problems.

Perhaps more than anything else, INTPs struggle in interpersonal situations involving strong displays of negative emotion. Such emotional displays can quickly unsettle INTPs, making them feel powerless and out of control. For instance, they often feel out of control when called upon to manage or mediate conflicts among young children. Since INTPs' typical style is to simply avoid interpersonal contact and thereby avoid conflict, they can feel clueless and paralyzed when it comes to handling external conflict.

INTPs also struggle with strong displays of negative emotions or perceived "neediness" from their romantic partners. When their partners, especially those with strong Fe expressiveness, come to them with an urgent need for support or reassurance, INTPs may find themselves feeling angry or spiteful rather than compassionate. This response is not intentional, but is more of a knee-jerk reaction stemming from feelings of powerlessness and ineptitude. This problem also ties into the fact that INTPs fail to experience empathy to the degree that Feeling types do. INTPs do not want to feign empathy, as it feels awkward and inauthentic. So all they feel capable of doing is proffering potential solutions in a Ti-Ne fashion, which may leave their support-seeking partner feeling frustrated and unsatisfied. This dissatisfaction may, in turn, further fuel INTPs' sense of spite and anger, since they feel they are being asked to function inauthentically and "out of their element."

In short, these sorts of situations highlight INTPs' Fe weaknesses and can quickly cause them to become hypersensitive and defensive. Indeed, whenever INTPs feel forced to deal directly with others' negative emotions, they are at high risk for losing control of themselves, which may include falling prey to their own "dark side."

Mimi : Debbie

2. GROWTH AND DEVELOPMENT

As discussed in my book, *The 16 Personality Types*, personality type development does not happen overnight. Rather, it is a gradual process of unfolding, propelled by life experiences and increasing self-awareness. Consequently, it can be helpful to analyze type development in terms of distinct, successive phases. In this chapter, we will explore three general phases of INTPs' growth and development.

Since personality development requires spending ample time in each phase before advancing to the next, we should resist the temptation to deem any phase inherently better or worse than another. We must remember that each phase of development is equally part of the human experience, guided by laws and forces that are to a certain extent beyond the control of the individual.

Phase I: Early Childhood

Early in life, perhaps even from birth, all personality types rely on the dominant function as their primary tool for navigating the world. My ISTP son, for instance, showed early signs of a dominant Ti. At around two years of age, with minimal prompting, he potty trained himself and stopped using his pacifier. At age five, he suddenly gave up soda, asserting it might hamper his development as a soccer player. In each of these cases, the results were immediate and lasting. This is the sort of thing that Ti does, independently making decisions and imposing disciplines on the self for the sake of achieving its goals.

It is not unusual for young INTPs to focus their Ti, which is a reductive function, on only one or two primary interests. They may use their Ti to master video games, collect and organize baseball cards, excel in school, develop strategies and methods to improve their sports performance, or, in the case of Einstein, to explore the nature of physical reality.

Since Ti is a Judging function, young INTPs may take themselves and their interests quite seriously. As we saw with my son, they may display precocious levels of self-discipline and self-control. They are often goal-oriented, striving for excellence in whatever captures their interests.

This is not to suggest that INTPs' inferior function is absent from Phase I. Indeed, Fe supplies the motivation for many of the young INTP's pursuits. They work hard to gain affirmation and recognition from their parents or peers (e.g., "Look what I can do!"). Their Fe may also manifest through the development of meaningful childhood friendships.

Phase II: Adolescence-30s

What distinguishes Phase II from Phase I is increasing polarity and conflict among the personality functions. INTPs can be seen as moving into Phase II when they experience a more pronounced conflict between the time and energy they devote to self (Ti) versus others (Fe). In Phase I, this is typically a non-issue, since they typically have plenty of time to enjoy both solitary (Ti) and social endeavors (Fe). Phase I INTPs are also not beholden to or responsible to anyone but themselves. They have relatively few obligations and are sheltered from the harsher realities and difficulties of life. But once INTPs reach adolescence and early adulthood, things begin to change, sometimes rather rapidly.

One of the biggest shifts involves a blossoming of INTPs' interest in romantic relationships. It's not that they are devoid of romantic thoughts or feelings in Phase I, but with the physiological changes of puberty, combined with cultural norms of mating behavior, INTPs start devoting more of their conscious attention to Fe matters. Indeed, it is not unusual for teenage INTPs to experience strong infatuation, even toward individuals they have hardly spoken to. This may be bolstered by a vivid fantasy life, which they use to escape reality and "get high" on romantic feelings. They may even use books, music, or movies to fan their romantic fantasies.

Because feelings can be so elusive, and therefore so mysterious and alluring, for INTPs, they may experience stronger crushes, fantasies, and infatuation than Feeling types do. Immersing themselves in feelings of love can feel nothing less than magical and intoxicating. Compared to their typical Ti mode of operating, such Fe dreaminess can seem an entirely new world. Psychologically speaking, discovering these strong feelings is in many regards a discovery of the "other half" of themselves.

As long as feelings of love and romance are confined to the imagination, INTPs really aren't at war with themselves. With relative ease, they can toggle between their Ti pursuits and their Fe fantasies. Once they become intent on actualizing their Fe fantasies, however, things become a lot trickier.

This surge of Fe focus may prove problematic for INTPs in several ways. Many young and naive INTPs, for instance, get lured into long-term relationships they later come to regret. By granting too much weight to their Fe infatuations, they make commitments that, in retrospect, their Ti struggles to justify.

An idealized Fe may also lead INTPs to adopt a sort of "grass is always greener" mentality toward their relationships. Since no partner could possibly live up to their romantic fantasies, INTPs may find themselves perpetually dissatisfied and looking for alternatives. They may jump from one relationship (or marriage) to the next as they desperately seek an elusive Fe ideal.

What may be the INTP's most difficult and recurrent struggle of all is balancing the time and energy invested in their Ti pursuits with that of their relationships. In our upcoming chapter on relationships, we will explore what I have framed as the "Lone Wolf vs. Mr. Nice Guy" dilemma, a scenario which can plague INTPs for decades.

As if all this wasn't enough, the effects of a hyperpolarized Fe is not limited to INTPs' relationships, but can also infiltrate their career decisions. For instance, Fe may lure INTPs into characteristically Feeling-oriented careers, such as human services or helping professions. Unfortunately, it is rarely long before INTPs working in these fields instinctively realize their work is too heavy on Fe. This, of course, is essentially the same problem that occurs when they enter into relationships based on feelings alone.

Phase II woes can be even worse for INTPs who experience a sort of Fe "double whammy," falling prey to Fe traps in both their careers and relationships. Unfortunately, this is not as uncommon as one might think. Such INTPs may try to assuage the resultant pain by drowning themselves in fantasies about more ideal careers or relationships.

Their Fe's desire to accomplish something big and important may add further fuel to INTPs' Phase II fire. Like other types, INTPs can be concerned with the advancement and promotion of their own ego. Male INTPs seem particularly concerned with making a name for themselves and leaving their mark on the world. So when their careers and relationships fall short of their ego's standards, they may become depressed or fall into addictive or otherwise unhealthy behaviors.

Phase III: 30s, 40s, & Beyond

If Phase II is like an emotional rollercoaster, replete with emotional highs and lows, Phase III is like being on emotional cruise control—a calmer, steadier, and more tranquil state of being. It in many ways resembles a sort of Zen-like existence.

Transitioning to Phase III can be a "two steps forward, one step back" type of affair. As is true of other types, INTPs don't skip over Phase II and move right into Phase III. Most will enjoy their fair share of pursuing, indulging, and promoting their Fe. Like other types, they need to dabble in "sin," including experiencing some of its negative consequences, before they are willing to earnestly explore alternatives. They need to explore and gratify their ego before they can open themselves to the prospect of letting go of it.

Indeed, from the vantage point of Phase II, Phase III may appear somewhat uninteresting or uneventful, similar to how a college student might view the life of an elderly person. Phase II INTPs may find it difficult to see how it is possible to be happy or stimulated in Phase III. They may worry about feeling bored or depressed, or that they will be forced to relinquish their cherished pursuits and interests. Fortunately, this is typically not required. The changes of Phase III are primarily psychological, involving a gradual shift in attitude and approach.

Phase III INTPs are typically less attached to their work in the sense that they are less concerned with the advancement or indulgence of their Fe ego. This allows them to enjoy their work for its intrinsic value, rather than obsessing over external "success." They also come to value and understand truth (T) and meaning (F) as a holistic experience, a way of being, rather than merely in terms of abstract ideas or concepts.

3. NEGATIVE POTENTIALS AND DISORDERS

We have already touched on certain INTP characteristics that might be negatively perceived by other personality types, such as their tendency to be aloof, self-absorbed, emotionally immature, or ineffective communicators. To be fair to INTPs, however, all personality types are immature, childish, and incompetent with respect to matters involving their inferior function. It just so happens that INTPs' Fe weaknesses are magnified in the interpersonal realm, making them more subject to public scrutiny.

In addition to bringing its own set of problems, the inferior function can also serve as a sort of gateway to a personality type's dark side or shadow. Moreover, individuals displaying a hyperpolarized relationship between their dominant and inferior function may exhibit characteristics of various psychological disorders.

In this chapter, we will explore what I will refer to as the "negative potentials" of the INTP personality type. This will include a discussion of the INTP's dark side, as well as various psychological disorders INTPs may be disposed to.

As will become evident in this chapter, I am generally uncomfortable with the frequency by which people are diagnosed with psychological "disorders." It has never been entirely clear to me where "normal" personality ends and "abnormality" begins. With certain exceptions, I am inclined to envision such matters as existing along a continuum rather than in discrete categories. Consequently, there may be times when, rightly or wrongly, I am accused of downplaying abnormality in favor of interpreting things according to degrees of normality.

The INTP's "Dark Side"

INTPs are typically fairly even-keeled and mild-tempered. They use their Ti to find strategies for minimizing stress and anxiety. This allows them to maintain a fairly neutral, perhaps even slightly optimistic mood, much of the time. When things are running smoothly, INTPs can handle most problems with relative ease.

There are situations, however, that cause INTPs' fragile and hypersensitive Fe to feel threatened or out of control. This may occur, for instance, when their romantic partners are finding fault with or "picking on them," rather than affirming or otherwise appeasing their Fe's "need to be needed."

As we saw in the previous chapter, INTPs may also lose decorum in situations involving strong expressions of negative emotions. Because INTPs are relatively ill-equipped to navigate emotionally-difficult situations, their inferior Fe is inclined to do all it can to defend itself. Hence, in emotionally intense or chaotic situations, INTPs may suddenly be overwhelmed with feelings of rage and anger, which, left unmitigated, may quickly transport them to the dark side.

When INTPs are enraged or angry, they think and act in irrational ways. They may, for instance, suddenly and unexpectedly lash out against a perceived perpetrator, such as a mate, child, or co-worker. In these unfortunate moments, INTPs may say or do things neither they nor others would ever expect from them. They may look and feel like they are possessed by something evil, that they are no longer themselves.

In many instances, INTPs manage to contain their anger, dealing with its effects on an inward basis. In contending with their own inner beast, they may experience any number of dark thoughts or urges. These may range from suicidal thoughts, to intense feelings of hatred, to fantasies of criminal acts. Generally, such thoughts are rather short-lived, truncated by a diminishment of the emotion, effective distractions, a return of Ti reasonability, or some combination thereof. But if INTPs dwell in darkness for any sustained period of time, they may find themselves in serious trouble. Of all types, they are probably the least likely to seek outside help, putting them at greater risk for becoming a victim of their own dark side.

Following such darker moments or periods, INTPs may feel some combination of guilt, confusion, fear, and concern. Discovering their dark potentials can be scary, as well as humbling. It forces them to acknowledge their weaknesses, including the fact that there are certain situations in which they are apt to lose control of themselves. *my mother*

Such experiences can also prompt them to think differently toward others. It can be easy for INTPs to project their distaste for neediness or dependency, expecting others to think and behave as they do. But once INTPs acknowledge lapses in their own self-control, they may become more forgiving and empathetic in this regard. They realize they can be just as mortal, just as fallible, or just as weak as the next person. *Yep!*

Suffering the trauma of their own dark side may also cause INTPs to lose some degree of faith in the potential for human betterment. They may feel that if they lack the requisite self-control to respond appropriately to stress, then it is unreasonable to believe that others will fare much better.

To minimize the likelihood of falling prey to their own dark side, INTPs first need to be aware of the causes and triggers of their dark emotions. This includes recognizing how their Fe hypersensitivity and insecurities may serve as a gateway to their dark side.

Second, INTPs need to stop listening to their dark emotions. As Thinking types, they must recognize that, outside of "fight or flight" emergencies, their emotions are rarely good compasses for navigating life. This is because many of their emotions, whether positive or negative, stem from the hypersensitivity or childishness of their inferior Fe. So in many ways, an INTP listening to his emotions is akin to taking advice from a naïve or angry child. If INTPs can avoid trusting and identifying with their dark emotions, they will incur far less collateral damage and return to a healthier state of mind more quickly. In lieu of buying into their emotions, INTPs are better off gathering all the pertinent information (Ne) and enlisting their Ti reasonability before acting or drawing conclusions.

Depression

Like other personality types, INTPs have the potential for depression. The precipitants of depression, however, will to some extent differ among the various types.

From a typological perspective, depression can result from functioning inauthentically with regard to one's type. For INTPs, this would involve living in such a way that their Ti and Ne are deprived of meaningful engagement. At first, Ti-Ne deprivation may produce feelings of dissatisfaction, apathy, or restlessness. But if this were to persist long enough, a more severe state of depression might ensue.

INTPs may also become depressed when they feel they have nothing important to contribute to the world or that the world doesn't really need them (Fe). Repeated "failures" or a persistent sense of hopelessness or dissatisfaction in their careers or relationships may prove especially difficult for INTPs to navigate.

Another common factor in INTP depression is their struggle with meaninglessness, the sense that life in general, or their lives in particular, are devoid of sufficient meaning. We will discuss INTPs' struggles with meaninglessness in greater detail in our next chapter.

Attention-Deficit Disorder (ADD)

In my experience, attention-deficit disorder (ADD) is most commonly diagnosed in NP types (especially ENPs), while attention-deficit hyperactivity disorder (ADHD) is most commonly diagnosed in SP types (especially ESPs). In both cases, it can be difficult to determine where normal type characteristics end and abnormal ones begin. After all, whenever individuals are immersed in circumstances that run counter to or fail to stimulate their natural tendencies and preferences (e.g., traditional schooling), they are bound to appear "out of place" or "abnormal." For instance, when NPs are expected to perform rote memorization or to learn in a linear fashion, or when SPs are expected to sit still and take in abstract ideas, there is a clear conflict between the methods and objectives of the educational system and those of the student.

Typically, INTPs appear less ADD-like (or what might be better described as more Ne-like) than ENPs. As dominant Thinkers, their ability to focus and "go inward" is generally sufficient to exempt them from the ADD classification. In some cases, ENTPs diagnosed with ADD may have mistyped themselves as INTPs, which could lead to an overestimation of the incidence of ADD among INTPs. While INTPs can be somewhat impulsive and distractible, they typically exhibit sufficient "executive control" to bring their mind into focus (Ti).

Autism/Asperger Syndrome

If ADD represents a sort of extreme right-brainedness, autism and Asperger syndrome would seem to fall toward the left-brain side of things. But if we roughly associate Ti with the left brain and Ne with the right brain, we might suspect that INTPs would fall somewhere in the middle (assuming their Ti wasn't overly dominant). It would therefore seem more likely that TJ types, especially STJs, who in my view are more consistently and characteristically left-brained, would cross over into autistic territory.

Simon Baron-Cohen has framed autism in terms of a strong preference for systemizing versus empathizing. If we use this criteria, we might be more inclined to associate the INTP personality type with autism. But again, most of the INTPs I have encountered seem more socially skilled (presumably due to their Ne and Fe) than certain ITJ individuals. This could of course be compromised in INTPs who struggle with social anxiety, but social anxiety is clearly a different animal than autism.

In light of the above, I suggest that INTPs may be more disposed to autism or Asperger's than some personality types, but I see no *a priori* reason to believe that INTPs would be more susceptible to autism or Asperger's than ISTPs or TJ types.

Narcissism

Narcissists are preoccupied with themselves, including their perceived level of power, status, prestige, and success. Some researchers have suggested that upwards of 75% of those with narcissistic personality disorder (NPD) are male, which seems consistent with common perceptions of narcissists.

Typically, narcissism is associated with extraversion, since extraverts, especially ESPs, seem more conscious of their image and appearance. But in his book, *Malignant Self Love: Narcissism Revisited*, Sam Vaknin distinguishes two types of narcissists: the somatic narcissist and the cerebral narcissist. While ESP narcissists would typically fall into the somatic category, Intuitive types, especially IN types, would tend toward the cerebral variety. According to Vaknin, cerebral narcissists seek to secure narcissistic supply by showcasing their knowledge, intellect, and intelligence. This might come, for instance, by way of academic, scientific, or scholarly achievement.

If we accept cerebral narcissism as a valid phenomenon, there is no reason to believe that INTPs would be immune from it. Indeed, they may even be more disposed to it because of their inferior Fe, which, as we've seen, can manifest as a desire to gain recognition and affirmation.

Vaknin also discusses how narcissists tend to devalue their romantic partners once the novelty of the relationship has worn off. This too would not seem uncommon for INTPs, since they can easily lose touch with their feelings of love and affection.

In sum, INTPs seem more inclined toward cerebral narcissism than most other types. While Vaknin sees the narcissist's chance of recovery as relatively slim, I tend to disagree, especially for those with milder cases. In my experience, as INTPs mature and develop, their need for ego affirmation gradually diminishes and is supplanted by a healthier sense of self-worth. Moreover, as we will see in our upcoming relationships chapter, there are ways in which INTPs can reframe their relationships so as to mitigate their tendency to devalue their partners.

Schizoid & Schizotypal Personality Disorders

Schizoid personality disorder (SPD) involves a diminished interest in interpersonal relationships, emotional coldness, and a preference for a secretive and solitary lifestyle. Based on this description, one can see why it is debatable whether SPD should be considered a disorder at all. Some have argued, for instance, that SPD differs little from an avoidant attachment style. Or, from a typological perspective, one might argue that it could be explained in terms of a strong preference for Introversion and/or Thinking. It should not surprise us, then, that

INTPs may resonate with many of the criteria and descriptions of the schizoid character. *Look up*

I tend to agree with the critics of SPD that it may not represent a disorder so much as a less common or less socially-endorsed personality style. INTPs should therefore avoid agonizing over the degree to which they fit the schizoid criteria. What really matters is that they are satisfied with their lives and their level of functioning.

INTPs seem less likely to fit the criteria for Schizotypal personality disorder, which involves odd, paranormal, or superstitious beliefs. This disorder is more closely related to schizophrenia, which occurs when individuals lose touch with concrete reality. I see schizophrenia as more likely to affect INJs, whose dominant N and inferior S might to some degree dispose them to a schizophrenic break between mind (N) and body (S). While INTPs may at times seem outwardly absent-minded, their tertiary Si typically keeps them sufficiently grounded to the concrete reality of the body.

4. QUESTING FOR TRUTH AND MEANING

We opened this book with the observation that INTPs feel they are on a quest to find truth and meaning. After a fairly lengthy detour in Chapters 1 -3, this chapter will pick up where we left off. In the first half of this chapter, we will consider the role of INTPs' inferior Fe with regard to their quest for meaning, as well as their meaning-related fears. We will also explore INTPs' struggle to find consistent sources of meaning. The second half of this chapter focuses on INTPs' search for convergent truth. This will include considering the effects of this search on their psychological well-being, as well as what a healthy approach to truth-seeking might look like for INTPs.

The Role of Fe in INTP's Quest for Meaning

Earlier in this book, I suggested that INTPs' concern for meaning is in many ways commensurate to their concern for truth, forming two sides of the same coin. In light of their status as Thinking types, their penchant for truth is clearly understandable, but why meaning? Isn't meaning more of an F issue? Here again, we must turn to the inferior function for an explanation.

Although Ti and Fe are often framed as opposing or opposite functions, they can also be viewed as complementary parts of a whole. From this perspective, we might say that truth (T) without meaning (F) or meaning without truth is incomplete and ultimately unsatisfying. This is why INTPs often insist that their Ti work feel meaningful. Without the meaning element, they feel that a critical piece of the puzzle is missing.

In the previous chapter, we saw how Fe can serve as a portal to INTPs' dark side. Here, I would like to point out how negative moods and emotions may also influence their perceptions of meaning. Namely, when INTPs are in a negative mood, they are more likely to struggle with concerns about meaninglessness. On rare occasions, some may even conclude that their lives have no potential for ever becoming meaningful.

Once again, the problem with this sort of thinking is it is founded on an irrational platform. When INTPs place their moods and emotions in high regard, they tend to get themselves into trouble. This is not to say that it is bad or unhealthy for INTPs to want their lives to feel meaningful. The problem is when they grant too much credence to extreme thoughts rooted in negative moods. And while shielding their thoughts from unwarranted emotional influence is easier said than done, this staple of cognitive therapy is one that INTPs, of all types, should be capable of mastering.

With that said, the prospect of meaninglessness can still be scary for INTPs. Indeed, this fear may be in large part what drives their quest for meaning. Without a sense of meaning and purpose, they may feel unmotivated and uninspired to seek truth. This is similar to an F type who feels that without a belief in truth, she will lack the inspiration to seek value and meaning.

Crises of Meaning

INTPs typically don't struggle with strong concerns about meaning-lessness until well into Phase II of their development. During that time, they often experience a sort of "crisis of meaning" that has a lasting effect on them. This is exemplified in the following excerpt from Russian novelist Leo Tolstoy:

> "The question, which in my fiftieth year had brought me to the notion of suicide, was the simplest of all questions... "What will come from what I am doing now, and may do tomorrow? What will come from my whole life?" otherwise expressed—"Why should I live? Why should I wish for anything? Why should I do anything?" Again, in other words: "Is there any meaning in my life which will not be destroyed by the inevitable death awaiting me?"

Here we see Tolstoy wrestling with the meaning of his own life in light of his future death. If death erases everything, is life really worth living? Is it worth all the effort and struggle?

Think this, all the time

For many individuals, such crises of meaning arise in the throes of loss or misfortune—a broken relationship, the loss of a job, an onset of illness, a succession of perceived failures, etc. For others, the crisis is more insidious, a slow realization that their lives have not materialized as they originally imagined. This often occurs around midlife, as the wonderment and idealism of childhood give way to the realities and challenges of adulthood.

For INTPs, intellectual exploration may be an equally potent factor in introducing questions regarding meaning, such as those pertaining to the nature or existence of God.

At some point in my early twenties, after careful study and examination, I disavowed the religion of my youth, concluding that its claims were self-contradictory and lacking sufficient evidence to earn my trust. This forced me to redirect my quest for truth and meaning, to look beyond traditional religion for answers to my questions. This included exploring the topic of meaning on its own terms.

Framing Meaning

While there is certainly no consensus on how to deal with meaning-related concerns, in his book, *Existential Psychotherapy*, Irvin Yalom offers a helpful framework for exploring these issues. Yalom posits two basic categories of meaning—galactic and terrestrial.

> *Galactic meaning*, or what we might also call abstract meaning, is what we commonly have in mind when considering "big questions" such as "What is the meaning of life?" or "Why are we here?" Many religions have tried to answer such questions through sweeping narratives about the origins, purpose, and destiny of the universe and humanity.

> *Terrestrial meaning*, by contrast, involves more concrete sorts of meaning. It's more about the experience of meaning than it is about answers to life's big questions. Terrestrial meaning emerges naturally as we go about our lives, pursuing our interests and satisfying our needs.

It's not that terrestrial meaning is wholly divorced from its galactic counterpart, since our beliefs and ideas invariably influence the way we experience life. Terrestrial meaning is important, however, because it reminds INTPs that meaning is not limited to grand ideas or meta-narratives. Even a complete absence of galactic meaning in the world would not preclude the existence of other sorts of meaning.

While it is certainly possible for INTPs to experience both types of meaning, those who are struggling to find galactic meaning can find terrestrial meaning an equally satisfying substitute. This is not to say that the process of transitioning from a galactic mindset to a terrestrial one is without its challenges, but it certainly can be done.

Related to this galactic-terrestrial dichotomy is the tension INTPs experience between reflecting on life (N) and acting in it (S). While they can certainly derive great pleasure from reflection and contemplation, there are times when they fatigue of thinking, feel they have reached a dead end, or just want to "get out of their own head." When this occurs, INTPs may struggle to find meaningful alternatives. Since their purpose and identity often revolve around N pursuits, they may view S activities as essentially pointless or mundane. This can create a situation in which their happiness seems to hinge almost entirely on the success of their N affairs. And since periods of inspiration and N success are bound to ebb and flow, they may find themselves trapped in a sort of bipolar existence—ecstatic one moment, down and depressed the next. Yep

Fortunately, such N-S, galactic-terrestrial struggles are a central theme of many existentialist philosophers, such as Nietzsche and Kierkegaard. Existentialists approach truth and meaning in a fairly terrestrial way, placing the burden of cultivating truth and meaning on the shoulders of the individual. They emphasize the importance of living honestly and authentically, of passionately pursuing one's interests and living out one's values. For those interested in further exploring existentialist thought, I highly recommend William Barrett's wonderful introduction to existential philosophy, *Irrational Man*, Colin Wilson's classic work, *The Outsider*, and Paul Tillich's gem, *The Courage to Be*.

Anxiety, Meaning, & "Being Okay"

To some extent, all INTPs struggle with anxiety. Anxiety may manifest as nervousness, muscle tension, worrisome thoughts, or various forms of social angst. Excessive anxiety can be mentally, physically, and emotionally draining, even debilitating. It can prove a real impediment to INTPs' work and relationships, not to mention their overall happiness and well-being.

A major source of an anxiety for INTPs is their fear of meaninglessness. In order to quell this fear, INTPs work hard to develop a meaningful philosophy of life, while also seeking work and relationships that bring meaning to their lives.

Another contributor to INTPs' anxiety is everyday worries, including concerns about money, work, and relationships. To assuage these concerns, INTPs may find it helpful to develop a philosophy along these lines: "Regardless of what happens, I will be okay." While this may at first sound a bit fluffy for the INTP, it actually has immense practical value. In many ways, believing they will be okay is no different from the belief that, regardless of circumstances, it will be possible for them to find or cultivate meaning.

With that said, there is a difference between giving lip service to the "I will be okay" concept and really knowing it. By "knowing it" I mean a deeper level of knowing, one that extends beyond mere cognitive acknowledgement. Developing this deep sense of assurance empowers INTPs to live courageously and authentically. It provides an antidote for fear, especially the fear of meaninglessness. If INTPs truly believe they have the skills and inner resources to be okay no matter what, life's trivial worries will lose their power over them.

To some extent, this deeper level of knowing emerges from life experience. For instance, as INTPs develop their niche skills and interests, they become increasingly confident in their ability to consistently procure meaning by way of "flow states." In such states, INTPs become deeply absorbed in their work and experience a sense of meaningful accomplishment. As they develop interests and methods that consistently induce flow, they naturally want to practice them more often. This generates a cycle of positive reinforcement, in which skills, interests, practice, and perceived meaning combine to produce more frequent and enduring flow experiences.

One can see this emphasis on the development of inner resources in Yogis and religious mystics. The underlying theory of their practices goes something like this: "If I can train my mind and body to be a perfect vessel for satisfying experience, then I will be protected against the vicissitudes of life that might otherwise threaten me." Those who successfully achieve this objective, such as Jesus or the Buddha, can then proclaim without hesitation that there is no reason to worry or be anxious. And while there are myriad ways INTPs can develop inner resources, the desired end remains similar to that of disciplines like Buddhism.

Although I have yet to embark on an exclusively "spiritual" path, I have incorporated certain disciplines and practices into my life that are meaningful to me in their own right, as well as helpful for becoming a better vessel for meaning and excellence. For those who are interested, these practices include:

- Getting adequate sleep (I rarely set an alarm)

- Writing every day, typically for at least two hours   *I need to*

- Yoga stretches and Feldenkrais movements

- Meditation

- Reading

- Jogging/walking

It may be worth mentioning that most of these are done spontaneously rather than on a scheduled basis. I perform them regularly, but mainly when I'm in the mood, which, thankfully, is fairly often. Writing is really my only scheduled activity in the sense that I do it first thing every morning (although I am also working to incorporate meditation into my morning routine). Not only have I found the above mind-body practices to be meaningful in their own right, but also valuable for releasing tension and curtailing anxiety.

In short, I think it is beneficial for INTPs to discover and oscillate among several options for experiencing concrete meaning, including relationships (which I could have also included on my list). That way, after fatiguing of one activity, there are other meaningful options waiting in the wings. I have sometimes thought of this in terms of "diversification of meaning."

Why INTPs Struggle to Find Convergent Truth

Even if INTPs were to relinquish their quest for galactic meaning, they might still seek hard truth to satisfy their thirst for inner order as exemplified in Einstein's famous assertion: "God does not play dice."

Despite their ostensible desire for convergent truth, INTPs find it difficult to consistently subscribe to any single theory. Indeed it is not uncommon for INTPs to require decades of exploration before making strong or consistent attestations of what they believe. In addition to the general problems faced by any truth-seeker, there are several potential reasons INTPs may struggle to "pin down" truth.

As we've seen, Ti and Ne can have a destabilizing effect, since both are adept at sniffing out exceptions, inconsistencies, and potential flaws. Ne may also incite INTPs to seek more and more information, *ad infinitum*. So in times when they fully submit to its whims and dictates, they often end up feeling lost and aimless, no closer to truth than when they started. While protracted exploration of options and alternatives may be less bothersome to ENTPs, for whom Ne is dominant, it can be prove unsettling to INTPs, whose Ti (and Fe) seeks a stronger sense of order and convergence.

INTPs can also get into trouble when they allow themselves to lose all faith at the first sign of an apparent exception. In my own investigations of typology, for instance, I was initially disillusioned by the lack of empirical data to support the existence of the cognitive functions and the functional stack. In fact, for a while, I was a critic rather than proponent of type theory. Fortunately, I remained open long enough to see the shortcomings of my initial concerns.

INTPs can also get stuck when they feel obliged to accept the pronouncements of those they see as respected authorities on a subject. INTPs assess whether an individual is learned and intelligent, and, if this proves to be the case, they may feel obligated, consciously or not, to accept his or her word on things. For instance, they may end up subscribing to moral or epistemological relativism, at least in part, because it is embraced by many modern intellectuals and academics. Unfortunately, INTPs who are too quick to sympathize with intellectual authorities may lose confidence in their own powers of reason and lose sight of the importance (and pleasure) of developing their own perspectives.

In short, INTPs walk a fine line between being too open and not open enough. On the one hand, they want to remain open because they enjoy the process of seeking and integrating new ideas (Ne). On the other hand, they can feel unsettled and disoriented when they become obsessed with seeking or questioning to the point of losing contact with their own reason (Ti) or with what they already know (Si).

Illusory Short-Cuts to Truth: Jumping the Stack

INTPs can appear bipolar in their search for truth. One day, they may be flying high, convinced they have finally found the answer, only to feel lost and aimless the next. This bipolarism tends to be most pronounced when INTPs set their sights on quickly finding answers to big and difficult questions. In such instances, they may feel incapable of doing anything else until they come to a firm conclusion about the issue at hand. And because INTPs rely on their philosophy of life as a platform for making decisions, they may also experience great confusion and ambivalence toward their careers and relationships. Indeed, when feeling lost as far as knowing themselves or their philosophy, they may feel paralyzed in all respects. They may feel they cannot function authentically until they have clearly defined who they are and what they believe.

When INTPs obsessively rush to make a decision or reach a conclusion, they are, in type speak, in the "grip of their inferior function." Elaine Schallock has also described this as "jumping the (functional) stack," involving an attempt to quickly leap from Ti to Fe, while effectively foregoing what may be a lengthy process of Perceiving in the middle

What is grip behavior?

I think this happens sometimes.

portion of their stack (Ne & Si). While problematic for myriad reasons, the impulsive nature of grip behavior can hinder INTPs' effectiveness as rational thinkers and decision-makers.

According to Schallock, a healthier way for INTPs to operate is to move from the top of the functional stack downward, including spending ample time in Perceiving mode. In Schallock's view, there is no quick or easy route to truth for INTPs. Rather, they must try on countless theories a la Ne before it becomes possible for them to reach an enduring degree of Fe conviction.

INTPs are wise to recognize the futility of impulsively seeking short-cuts to truth. As Schallock suggests, they need ample time to test and experiment with a breadth of theories and ideas (Ne), not to mention sufficient life experience (Si), before forming anything resembling an enduring theory or philosophy (Fe). They can therefore benefit from exercising patience and learning to enjoy the seeker's journey, rather than falling for illusory short-cuts.

It may also help INTPs to remember that they are not J-types. It is the job of J-types to know or proffer answers (i.e., by way of Te or Fe) earlier in life. The INTPs' role, as a P-type, is to explore and proffer questions or ideas (Ne), not deliver immediate Fe answers. But because their Fe compels them to seek convergent answers, it can be easy for INTPs to assume that Fe answers are what the world wants or needs from them. They may assume that the world has no use for their questions, their skepticism, or their Ne creativity. But these assumptions are merely projections of their inferior function. The truth is that the world needs them to ask probing questions, to poke holes in existing theories, and to provide creative or explorative "food for thought." Indeed, the INTP's role, especially early in life, more closely resembles that of the artist, skeptic, critic, or provocateur than that of the sage or prophet.

Remembering these things may help INTPs be more patient and comfortable leaving their ideas open-ended. Sure, they will gradually

I've figured out this doesn't work.

develop and refine their understanding of themselves and their interest areas over time, but they are wise to resist the allure of the "shotgun approach," in which they try to get things settled all at once.

INTPs might also be wise to remind themselves that, even if they were to achieve their desired answers, they would soon be looking for new problems to explore. So if the overall point is for INTPs to engross themselves in stimulating and meaningful explorations, what is the point of trying to rush to conclusions?

Closing Thoughts

INTPs are prone to placing big demands on themselves when it comes to truth and meaning. This is exemplified in their quest for a "theory of everything," as well as for an ideal philosophy of life. This, combined with their desire to make an impact and enjoy intellectual success, can make their quest a rather high-minded and unrealistic one. Granted, INTPs still need some sort of identity and direction in life. Without an orienting direction, it is easy for them to feel lost, aimless, and useless. For this reason, developing a suitable career or vocation can seem of great importance to INTPs. But before we dive into INTP career issues, we will first take some time to explore some of their political, religious, and philosophical inclinations.

5. POLITICAL, RELIGIOUS, AND PHILOSOPHICAL PROPENSITIES

Personality type influences the way we see the world. It shapes our beliefs, values, interests, and aversions. It also plays a substantial role in determining our political, religious, and philosophical preferences. The study of the effects of psychology on beliefs and worldview is called psychoepistemology. Research has shown that different personality types display different "psychoepistemological profiles." For instance, different types will vary in the degree to which they prefer a metaphoric versus empirical versus rational style of knowing.

In this light, INTPs, like other types, are typically misguided in viewing their approach as immune to subjective bias. While it is true that certain beliefs are more valid or accurate than others, all types gravitate toward certain values and assumptions that jive with the functions of their functional stack. We might even suggest that each function has its own set of values and preferred ways of seeing things.

In this chapter, we will explore some of INTPs' political, religious, and philosophical inclinations. This will include an assessment of the relative contributions of their four functions to the way they see and understand the world.

Political Propensities

Ti and Ne might well be viewed as "freedom-seeking" functions, contributing to the INTP's status as the most fiercely independent of all types. Indeed, INTPs deplore being told what to do or how they should do something. They want to do things their own way and in their own time. This can inspire them to resist or rebel against, even if only inwardly, various rules, laws, and authorities perceived as potential threats to their freedom and autonomy. These threats may come in the form of governmental or corporate power; INTPs are wary of both. Consequently, almost all INTPs, at least at some point in their lives, will gravitate toward some sort of anarchist or libertarian philosophy.

The fact that INTPs are Introverts and use Si can contribute to a propensity toward material and fiscal conservativism. Like other Si types, INTPs are bothered by perceived wastefulness or squandering of natural resources (especially non-renewable ones). Therefore, many INTPs have a strong environmentalist or conservationist streak.

Fiscally speaking, INTPs are prone toward skepticism of social programs, although not necessarily all of them. This may stem from a confluence of several factors: their Ti distrust in the efficacy of collective programs, their Ti preference for individual-driven solutions, their Si fiscal conservatism, and their relative lack of Fi sympathy for niche causes.

Therefore, in considering INTPs' top three functions, we might well expect them to gravitate toward some form of libertarian philosophy, perhaps combined with certain environmental and corporate regulations. But there is one more function we must discuss, which, as we've seen, often exerts more power and influence than we might expect. Indeed, the influence of Fe on INTP political leanings cannot be overlooked.

Fe can be understood as the function of democracy, as well as socialism. Einstein himself was a socialist at heart. Fe is concerned with the common good, the welfare of all. In INTPs, Fe can imbue an almost mystical sense of love and concern for the general welfare of humanity. In fact, some INTPs seem more concerned about the welfare of humanity in general than the welfare of their own family. Again, Einstein was an apt example of this.

With that said, most INTPs don't latch onto democratic or socialist ideals and never look back. Eventually, Ti and Ne creep back in and start questioning the practical merits of these collective, centralized systems. For instance, INTPs may question the value of democracy in a society where people assume a "herd mentality" and fail to think for themselves. They may come to see both top-down authoritarian rule, as well as bottom-up democratic processes, as inherently flawed.

In the end, many INTPs fall into a state of political cynicism or apathy, opting to go about their business without much hope in collective solutions. Typologically, we might interpret this as their Ti regaining control, focusing on its own affairs, and placing little stock in Fe solutions. INTPs differ from INTJs in this respect. INTJs, such as Al Gore, are more likely to be consistently politically active, since their Te is always looking for ways to make external systems more rational.

Religious Propensities

The same dynamics hold for INTPs' religious preferences as we saw with their political ones. Namely, their first inclination is to shuck all authority. For many INTPs, this makes theism an unacceptable option, explaining why INTPs are so common among atheists and agnostics. This is not to suggest that INTPs forsake theism without some rational justifications for doing so. There are plenty of sound arguments, particularly those related to the problem of evil, against the existence of an omnipowerful, omniscient, and/or omnibenevolent god. What I want to emphasize, however, is that INTPs' personality type makes them more prone to seeking out and embracing these arguments. If we are being honest, INTPs can be so hell-bent on being free and independent that they don't want to be accountable to anyone or anything, including an all-powerful deity. This is not to suggest that INTPs are somehow amoral or immoral, but only that they want to be in charge of themselves.

Although there are plenty of INTP non-theists, many INTPs will, to some degree, stay connected to organized religion in some way, shape, or form. This too can be explained in terms of their inferior function. As we've seen, Fe is concerned about the common good. It is therefore not difficult to see how, for instance, Jesus's message of love, acceptance, and forgiveness might appeal to INTPs' Fe. This is especially true if his message is interpreted as entailing an all-inclusive and all-encompassing love, a love that is big enough to save all of humanity. Universal love and salvation are clearly Fe ideals.

Fe may also encourage INTPs to continue religious participation for social and emotional reasons. The notion of "community" is another Fe ideal that can appeal to INTPs. The idea of being intimately and emotionally connected to a group of people can be enticing and comforting to INTPs' Fe. Adding to this are feelings of mysticism commonly evoked by religious settings. Music, in particular, can have a powerful effect on INTPs, stirring their Fe in what can feel like divine and powerful ways. Hence, organized religion has multiple channels for inducing an Fe euphoria potent enough to keep them coming back.

More subtle feelings of mysticism, or what INTP Immanuel Kant referred to as sense of the sublime, are also common among INTPs. Einstein often described his sense of awe and wonder toward life and the universe. And because INTPs are terrified at the prospect of meaninglessness, they may work to augment such mystical feelings through spiritual practices, or roll them into some sort of metaphysical philosophy, such as pantheism. Indeed, many INTPs are drawn to the notion of an immanent spirit or force that animates the universe.

Such a philosophy has the advantage of not being coercive (i.e., not conflicting with their Ti), while at the same time seeming more meaningful than a spiritless atheism. This is why many INTPs take interest in Eastern philosophies and practices, such as Buddhism.

Buddhist practice, which for our purposes I will more or less equate with meditation, has many Ti elements. It requires independent practice and careful attention to one's thoughts. It uses subjective experiences and observations to understand how the mind works on a practical level, particularly its contributions to human suffering (or happiness).

Phase II INTPs may dabble in meditation, but often don't have the patience to take it seriously. Since meditation promises little in the way of extrinsic ego rewards, it is really more of a Phase III endeavor. Phase II INTPs who do manage to meditate regularly will likely reach Phase III more quickly than those who don't. Regardless, I see meditation as an ideal practice for INTPs, providing them a first-hand glimpse into the workings of the mind, not to mention a potential path to enlightenment.   *fuck ↑ Meditation*

Philosophical Propensities

Modern philosophy is commonly divided into two main schools: analytic philosophy and continental philosophy. Although this division is far from being clear-cut, I will argue that INTPs generally gravitate more toward the continental camp.

Analytical philosophy is ahistorical. Its focus is more precise and narrow than that of the continental ilk. Namely, it is concerned with carefully analyzing the language, logic, and grammatical structure of sentences and propositions. Through the analytic process, analytical philosophers believe that truth will be laid bare.

Analytical philosophy can also be tied to logical positivism and science. Its positivism derives from confidence in the analytic method, as well as the scientific method, to reveal certain truth. Considering its concern for precision and formal analysis, and its strong sympathies toward science, we might roughly associate the analytical school with Extraverted Thinking (Te).

The continental school, by contrast, has more of a Ti-Fe and Ne-Si feel to it. According to *The Cambridge Dictionary of Philosophy*, after World War II, continental philosophy was more or less synonymous with phenomenology. Phenomenologists believe that certain truths can be known through introspection and self-observation, which certainly has a Ti ring to it. But even broader than that, continental philosophy relates to an interest in developing a "philosophy of life," or what we might call a human-centered philosophy (Fe). This is also where continental philosophy merges with existential philosophy, which wrestles with concerns over meaning and the human condition.

Continental philosophy also entails historical and cultural elements, namely, an interest in the history (Si) and evolution (Ne) of ideas over time. There is thus a sense of openness, fluidity, and relativism, at times even tentativeness, in the continental school, which is less obvious in the analytic school. Continental thinkers are more dialectical in their writing (Ne-Fe), engaging and interacting with the ideas of others, as though having an imagined conversation or debate. For them, truth, at least the sort of truth that they view as meaningful to human life, is worked out through a combination of individual reasoning (Ti) and human dialogue (Ne-Fe).

With that said, INTPs are still predominantly inner Judgers (Ti). As we saw in the previous chapter, they are not always comfortable leaving matters entirely open-ended. In this respect, they may be somewhat less inclined toward the freewheeling methods of Ne, preferring instead to try to hammer down truth in the spirit of the analytic thinker. Hence, the degree to which INTPs focus on hard truths and methods versus softer ones will depend on the individual INTP, as well as where she is at in her philosophical journey.

6. CAREERS, MAJORS, AND INTERESTS

As dominant Thinkers, INTPs naturally grant greater priority to their work (Ti) than their relationships (Fe). Indeed, it may be an understatement to suggest that, for INTPs, work is a big deal. Unfortunately, perhaps more than any other type, the road to satisfying work can be a rough and rocky one for INTPs. As we've seen, INTPs often feel they must thoroughly understand themselves, as well as their talents and abilities, before settling into a career. But because pinning down a sense of self or purpose can be tricky business, matching self with career is rarely as easy for INTPs as it might seem.

Another complicating factor is INTPs' rugged individualism and unconventionalism. INTPs deplore doing things in standard, predefined ways. As Ti-Ne types, standardization runs against their grain. INTPs thrive on doing things their own way, developing and employing their own Ti approach. This makes them reluctant to function as employees, loathing the idea of answering to someone else. INTPs also struggle to embrace an organization's vision and methods as their own. In many respects, they are control freaks. They want to be in full control of themselves and avoid being controlled or managed by others.

INTPs are also sensitive to what they see as meaningless or menial aspects of a given job. They can be resistant to what they see as excessive or unnecessary administrative work, or what is commonly called bureaucracy or "red tape."

Time is another factor. INTPs often need a great deal of time to explore and experiment with their interests before anything resembling a clear vocational vision begins to emerge. While geniuses like Einstein may discern their path rather quickly, for most INTPs, it can take years, even decades, before things come together with greater clarity.

Career Choice: Journey or Destination?

In light of the above, selecting a career or college major can be a scary and tenuous affair for INTPs. They may fear that making the wrong choice may doom them to a life of misery performing uninspiring work. They may also worry that choosing a vocational direction means committing themselves to a rather narrow set of interests and activities.

Without downplaying the perceived importance of well-informed career decision-making for INTPs, I am going to go out on a limb and suggest that their initial choice of career or college major may not be as critical or confining as they might imagine.

Why do people in general, and INTPs in particular, consider it so important to choose the ideal career or major upfront? In large part, this belief relates to our tendency to think of ourselves, as well as our careers, in terms of fixed, static categories. We might think of ourselves as having a defined structure and careers as having their own particular structure. So once we feel we have adequately defined ourselves, we go about searching for careers that are a good "fit" or "match."

As an INTP, I certainly understand the desire to find the perfect self-career congruence. But having lived long enough to observe how individuals operate in their careers, it seems that taking the first step in a given vocational direction is more like beginning a journey than it is arriving at a final destination. Viewed this way, the first career step, while determining one's general direction (e.g., north, west, east, or south), is often far less restrictive or prescriptive than we might think.

Furthermore, careers are often not what we imagine them to be. Again, this is largely due to the fact that we tend to imagine them in black-and-white, abstract terms. In my view, most career fields are broad enough to accommodate a breadth of personality types. There is no *a priori* reason to believe INTPs could not find ways of functioning authentically in any number of career fields. And even if there isn't an obvious, predefined niche for the INTP, it doesn't mean that one cannot be discovered or created.

As INTPs gain experience in a given career field, they become increasingly capable of functioning creatively within that field. Accrued knowledge and experience are precursors to vocational freedom, ingenuity, and innovation. Only by understanding *what is* does it become possible to effectively envision what *could or should be*. Such is the beauty of combining expertise with ingenuity.

Despite this, many individuals, especially idealistic N types (including INTPs), opt to ignore their current or past career course in favor of dreaming about more ideal alternatives. They fail to see that it is not necessarily the career that is most important, but the way they function with respect to that career. Given sufficient background knowledge, INTPs could feasibly apply their Ti and Ne to nearly anything.

Among INTPs' signature strengths are creativity and ingenuity. While these traits may make it difficult for them to readily conform to pre-existing standards, they can be a boon for INTPs willing to think outside the box and carve out their own niche. Building a career around oneself, could there be anything better for an INTP?

All of this is not to say that INTPs should or should not obtain a college degree. As we've seen, expertise is in many ways a prerequisite for creative innovation. A college education represents one viable path for INTPs to begin acquiring the necessary knowledge and expertise in a given discipline.

INTP Personality Functions in Career Selection

Unlike SJ and TJ types, INTPs are not all that keen on designing or executing highly formalized experiments. Seeking hard facts through controlled experiments is largely a Te enterprise. INTPs are more interested in applying reason to analyze or hone concepts, theories, or methods (Ti), as well as in making connections between existing theories and concepts (Ne). Here again Einstein's example proves useful. Even though Einstein was a scientist, much of his work was done independently, in his own mental laboratory. Like Einstein, many INTPs prefer to use their own methods and "thought experiments" for discerning truth, rather than functioning as "professional" scientists.

Ne involves an open-ended exploration of ideas, lending itself to the arts, entrepreneurship, inventorship, as well as scholarship. As an open-ended Perceiving function, Ne is comfortable with ambiguity, seeing ideas as fluid and contextual. Consequently, many subjects in the humanities (e.g., religion, philosophy, history, literature, languages), as well as journalism, can be good fits for NP types.

Since Ti is paired with Fe in their functional stack, INTPs are often, though certainly not always, drawn to human systems and subjects (Fe)—psychology, the humanities, social sciences, etc. However, because they still seek what we might call "harder" sorts of truth (static concepts, theories, frameworks, etc.), many fail to feel entirely at home in the more open-ended humanities.

Fe may also compel INTPs to pursue interests similar to those of ENFJs, for whom Fe is the dominant function. Namely, ENFJs often serve as teachers and counselors. They love providing counsel and advice to help others improve their lives. Similarly, INTPs may fancy themselves wise philosophers. They may dream of a career where they can seek wisdom and use it to counsel or advise others.

Unfortunately, INTPs obsessed with their Fe may overlook potentially good career options because, on the surface, they seem too far removed from their preferred source of validation—people. Many INTPs cater to their Fe by selecting people-oriented work, such as healthcare, teaching, counseling, etc. And while people-oriented careers are certainly appealing to their Fe, it is rarely long before INTPs realize the inherent strain of constantly engaging with others. Therefore, they are typically better off selecting careers that heavily utilize Ti and Ne and don't require too much in the way of direct Fe engagement.

Independent Experiments

INTPs enjoy collecting information, as well as personally experimenting with it, for the sake of discovering practical or theoretical truths. They often function like phenomenologists, learning by studying the workings of their own minds. What follows is a sample of some independent experiments an INTP might conduct:

- Exploring the effects of various meditation techniques

- Experimenting with the workings of their own bodies (e.g., Feldenkrais, yoga, martial arts, etc.)

- Engineering mindbody or cognitive-behavioral techniques for reducing pain, depression, or anxiety

- Philosophically wrestling with the mind-body problem

- Considering unconventional ways of improving or enhancing their relationships

Many of these examples highlight INTPs' interest in self-help and self-exploration. They are always looking for ways of optimizing and improving things, including themselves. As mentioned in the Introduction, INTPs commonly think of themselves as instruments. By working to understand and fine tune themselves (Ti), they feel they might also contribute something worthwhile to the collective (Fe).

Having established the fact that INTPs relish independent investigations, the looming question is how they can make money doing so. Indeed, there may be nothing INTPs want more than to get paid for doing what they love. Toward this end, many work to develop and utilize what we will call "marketable skills."

Marketable Skills

Much to their dismay, INTPs don't get paid merely for thinking, questioning, or experimenting. This leaves them with two basic options. The first is to work a day job for income and forgo commercializing their primary interests. The second option, which we will now discuss, is to develop marketable skills that can be used to enhance, market, or commoditize their work.

Shaping their work into a marketable product or service can be a frustrating affair for INTPs, since doing so can make them feel they are compromising the purity of their work. At the same time, INTPs don't want their work going forever unnoticed or unrecognized, which may compel them to find a channel for bringing it to the world.

In many cases, one marketable skill is not enough. Unless recognized as unusually brilliant, an INTP writer may not only need to hone her writing talents, but must also learn the ins and outs of blogging, publishing, email marketing, search engine optimization, etc. Viewed from the front end, this could easily be perceived as an overwhelming, and therefore unappealing, enterprise for INTPs. They might wonder how it is possible to develop their desired level of expertise while being forced to function as a "jack of all trades." Indeed, when forced to devote time and energy to too many things at once, INTPs can get weary and lose sight of their primary interest. It is therefore imperative that they exercise patience to allow adequate time for exploring their primary interests and developing their primary skills. By staying rooted in this way, they can avoid the sense of overwhelm that comes from trying to tackle too many things at once.

What follows is an overview of three types of marketable skills INTPs may find useful across a variety of settings, whether working as employees or freelancers:

IT / Computers

Because of their gift of intuitive logic, most INTPs have a knack for learning and understanding computers and information systems. With that said, those without a natural interest in computer science may drag their feet if they don't have another reason for learning a given program or system. Such INTPs may opt to delay their learning until motivated by a real-world application. Nonetheless, it goes without saying that technical know-how remains an invaluable skill in today's marketplace.

Writing / Blogging

Most INTPs are better than average writers. Unfortunately, many fail to recognize this about themselves, since they often compare their writing talents to those of the more flowery F types. But not all writing needs to be flowery. INTPs are particularly skilled with writing in clear and accessible ways. They are good at discerning "what is essential" (Ti) and communicating that information in interesting (Ne) and digestible (Fe) ways. Writing is also one of the best ways for INTPs to explore and share their ideas. Therefore, choosing a college major that develops and enhances their writing skills, such as journalism or the humanities, may prove beneficial.

Blogging can serve as an excellent platform and motivator for INTPs to wrestle with and hone their ideas, as well as their writing talents. It can be particularly appealing to INTPs because a blog is by nature a "work in progress." Blogging doesn't require one to get everything right upfront (as might feel necessary, for instance, when publishing a book), but is amenable to continued modification as new insights and experiences unfold. Hence, with time and practice, INTPs can develop greater expertise in their chosen subject area, while also becoming more confident and proficient as writers.

Business / Marketing / Entrepreneurship

INTPs are natural entrepreneurs in the sense of wanting to work independently. The great thing about entrepreneurship is it affords complete control over one's work. The potential downside, as we've discussed, is entrepreneurs may feel obliged to wear too many different hats.

Since money is rarely a primary motivator for INTPs, they often shy away from majoring in business and marketing. Interested in the abstract and theoretical, business can seem a bit mundane and commonplace for their taste. As with computer applications, INTPs may therefore avoid studying business and marketing until it proves absolutely necessary. Fortunately, for modern-day INTPs, marketing can be accomplished straight from their laptop, without ever having to leave their seat or pick up a phone.

The Value of a "Day Job"

While INTPs may dream of being freed from the shackles of scheduled work, a day job can often be a blessing in disguise for INTPs. I'm not suggesting that INTPs should put their nose to the grindstone for 60 hours a week and ignore their primary interests. Part-time work, however, can serve as a nice complement to their personal projects.

If we're being honest, it is difficult for most INTPs to perform focused intellectual or creative work for much more than six hours a day. So by working a day job for four or five hours a day, INTPs aren't really losing much as a far as productive time. In fact, a day job may even help focus their energies, knowing they have a set block of time to devote to their studies or creative work.

A day job can also force INTPs to get out of their heads and engage with others. This can serve to elevate their mood, which can tend toward the depressive when they spend too much time alone. Periods of "people time" can be enjoyable for INTPs, stimulating both their Ne and Fe.

Ideally, an INTP day job would be fairly stress-free, but not overly mundane. It might involve some combination of light physical work and working with people. It would also prove sufficient to pay the bills, while granting ample free-time to explore their passions. Potential options might include working as a waiter, barista, bartender, mechanic, construction worker, UPS driver, etc. Or, for INTPs with a professional degree, working as a part-time employee might be a good option.

Recognizing the value of some degree of scheduled work can help INTPs let go of the idea that only full-time solitary work will be acceptable. To the contrary, INTPs are typically happier when they partake in a variety of activities each day, thereby satisfying all their functional needs—T, N, S, and F. Granted, there is a pecking order for these functions, but as P-types, INTPs need variety to remain happy, stimulated, and balanced.

Impulsivity, Achievement, & Mastery

A commonly overlooked factor in INTP career issues is their
impulsivity. Instead of waiting patiently for future rewards, impulsive
individuals tend to seek quicker and more immediate gratification.
Impulsivity has been correlated with Extraversion, Thinking, and
Perceiving. So although INTPs may not be as impulsive as say, ENTPs
might be, many display significant levels of impulsivity.

Another important factor in INTP careers is their desire for
achievement and recognition. Rightly or wrongly, they may feel that
doing something big is the only way to make their mark on the world,
the only way to prove their worth. When combined with impulsivity,
a thirst for achievement can engender a sense of hurriedness and
urgency in INTPs, the sense that time is working against them. They
may feel that if they don't work hard and fast enough, they will never
contribute anything valuable to the world.

This urgent push for achievement is often counterbalanced by INTPs'
concern for mastery, expertise, and quality work. As Introverts, they
are repelled by shoddy work whose primary purpose is to make
money. They bemoan the practices of "disposable culture," where
things are made quickly and cheaply, without concern for quality or
durability. INTPs prefer the idea of producing something of lasting
worth, rooted in mastery (or at least competence) in a given discipline.

So what are impulsive, achievement-oriented, and mastery-oriented
INTPs to do? How can they balance these things in a satisfying and
effective way?

There are many ways INTPs can reduce impulsivity and improve their
focus and perseverance. To some extent, developing and committing
to meaningful and achievable goals will naturally enhance their
powers of focus. They can also employ various cognitive and
behavioral strategies to reduce anxiety and distractions, including
simple practices like turning off the phone, foregoing the temptation

to check email or social media, and finding a work setting that provides optimal stimulation for creative work. INTPs can also benefit from crafting a lifestyle that routinely affords them large blocks of time to focus on their work.

An alternative strategy might involve reframing their career goals in light of their impulsive tendencies. They might, for instance, reimagine their career in terms of a series of smaller, loosely related projects, rather than obsessively searching for a more grandiose career or project. Doing so might require them to take themselves and their careers a little less seriously, tweaking their self-image to better reflect the reality of their natural tendencies. Of course, settling for a less grandiose career can be a difficult thing for many INTPs to swallow, especially for those with big ideals. Consequently, many will resist this approach, opting instead to continue their search for an "ideal" career.

Subjectivity vs. Objectivity in INTP Careers

Since truth and accuracy are important to INTPs, they often stop to consider (or reconsider) the philosophical foundations of their work. Their goal is to ensure they are approaching things in the right way and have clarified their theoretical and conceptual platform.

Unfortunately, discerning the "right" or "ideal" philosophical platform is no easy task. Philosophers may spend their entire lives studying these issues without arriving at firm conclusions. This can be troubling for INTPs, who, as we've seen, seek a solid platform of truth for their lives and work. They are thus left with the choice of continuing to wrestle with philosophical issues versus moving forward in absence of complete certainty.

INTPs may explore different ways of circumventing this problem. They may opt to focus more on the degree to which their work makes them happy versus fretting over its objective value or validity. INTP writers, for instance, may work to balance the subjective enjoyment of the writing process with the time required to provide accurate content.

We might also consider whether typology provides any insight into these issues. Namely, are INTPs better off adopting a Ti focus, focusing primarily on activities that enhance their own subjective happiness? Or, should they keep at least one eye focused on the objectivity (Fe) of their approach?

If we adopt the view that it is best for each personality type to work from the top of the functional stack downward and to focus primarily on engaging the dominant and auxiliary functions, it does not seem unreasonable to suggest that INTPs are justified in emphasizing the subjective elements of their work. While Ti is concerned with objective truth, it is characteristically subjective in its workings, doing things in its own idiosyncratic way rather than relying on collective methods or endorsements. Ne also seems less objective and more divergent in its functioning. So it appears that, according to the upper half of INTPs' functional stack, they may be wired to function more like artists or innovators than conventional scientists.

Another way of framing the subjectivity-objectivity issue is recognizing that the good life is comprised of the good, the true, and the beautiful. So rather than focusing exclusively on objective truth, INTPs might think of their work in terms of its subjective truth, beauty, or goodness. Those looking for a champion of the aesthetic approach can find one in Nietzsche, who famously framed life in general, as well as his own life in particular, as "a work of art."

Holland Interests & Careers

Formal career assessments generally include three primary measures: personality, abilities, and interests. In this section, we will explore some of INTPs' common interest areas, as well as various careers and majors associated with those interests.

To aid and orient our discussion, we will draw on six interest themes described by John Holland. These include Realistic (R), Investigative (I), Artistic (A), Social (S), Enterprising (E), and Conventional (C) interests, or what are collectively dubbed "RIASEC."

After identifying an individual's top two or three interest domains, the letters can be combined in a way similar to the personality types to form a multi-letter Holland Code (e.g., IAS, RAI). This can then be matched with careers associated with that particular Holland code. Websites like O*Net, for instance, have a large database of careers that have been assigned a three-letter Holland code.

Realistic (R)

Individuals with Realistic interests enjoy physical, hands-on work, often involving machines (e.g., repairing vehicles, tinkering with computers, construction). They typically prefer working with "things" more than with people. It is therefore unsurprising that this interest domain is correlated with a preference for Thinking over Feeling. Sensing and Perceiving types are also somewhat more inclined toward Realistic work than are Intuitives or Judgers.

Realistics are often visual or kinesthetic learners, commonly excelling in spatial visualization. Those with strong spatial-visualization skills tend to do well with schematic charts and diagrams, as well as envisioning and mentally rotating three-dimensional objects.

The following Realistic careers may be suitable for some INTPs:

- Mechanic

- Computer/electronics repair

- Electrician

- Horticulture

- Various "day jobs" (see above)

Investigative (I)

The Investigative domain is typically a top preference among INTPs, involving analytic, scientific, academic, and related pursuits. Investigative types may enjoy working with ideas, theories, or data. They often prefer Thinking over Feeling and Intuition over Sensing. They perform particularly well on the mathematics portion of aptitude tests.

We will discuss Investigate careers according to five general categories: the hard sciences, social sciences, computer science, scholarship, and freelance investigations.

The "Hard" Sciences

While there is no absolute difference between the hard sciences (e.g., chemistry) and the soft sciences (e.g., sociology), the hard sciences are presumed to deal with more clear-cut, unequivocal facts. This is due to the fact that the physical world, at least in the Newtonian sense, is less variable and less complex than the psychosocial world of human beings, making it easier to study and describe with certainty.

One hard science that is likely to appeal to INTPs is theoretical physics. Much of theoretical physics, particularly that involving quantum mechanics, seems no simpler or easier to describe than human behavior. Because of the elusive and somewhat unpredictable nature of the quantum world, INTPs may find it a deeply interesting field of study.

With regard to other hard sciences, INTPs may be less enthusiastic. One reason for this is the hard sciences seem relatively unrelated to INTPs' concern for "how to live." In other words, they may seem too disconnected from human problems. INTPs may also find the methodologies of the hard sciences overly tedious or exacting. As we've seen, INTPs would rather work with concepts and ideas than fuss over precise measurements and data collection.

This is not to say, however, that INTPs can never find a satisfying niche in the hard sciences, even if it means functioning largely as interpreters, synthesizers, or popularizers. INTPs do like the idea of discovering and promoting hard truth. But they also want their work to be interesting and meaningful which, at least for some INTPs, involves work that somehow links up with human beings. Hence, fields like biology, physiology, or neuroscience may be of greater appeal than physics or chemistry for many INTPs.

The Social / Moral Sciences

INTPs may also enjoy working in the social sciences (history, economics, psychology, sociology, geography, anthropology, archeology, political science, etc.). Unlike the hard sciences, the social sciences seem more conducive to INTPs' interests in human nature. The same is true for the avant-garde field of moral science.

While the disciplinary boundaries of moral science have yet to be clearly demarcated, I see moral science as encompassing work in positive psychology, various types of ethics (e.g., population ethics, neuroethics), happiness studies, communication and peace studies, etc. Some of the major players in this field are Mihalyi Csikszentmihalyi, Martin Seligman, Jonathan Haidt, Daniel Goleman, the Dalai Lama, and, more recently, Sam Harris.

Moral science exists at the interface of science, psychology, and philosophy. It considers how human beings might live better lives, both individually and collectively. In his recent book, *The Moral Landscape*, Sam Harris argues that discussions of morals and ethics should be framed exclusively in terms of human well-being. He also suggests that human well-being can be studied empirically and scientifically, making it more than a subjective or religious topic. By approaching morality more objectively, Harris sees it possible to surmount many of the subjective differences and biases among individuals and cultures, allowing humanity to make moral decisions based on evidence rather than custom or tradition.

With that said, INTPs will likely have mixed feelings toward moral science. On the one hand, their Ti may balk at the notion of externally-prescribed moral standards. They may worry that moral science could eventually impinge on human freedom. On the other hand, INTPs do believe that some ways of living are superior to others and, therefore, that some degree of objectivity does apply to the moral realm.

As with the hard sciences, INTPs may be slow to invest significant time and energy exploring a rather narrow set of social or moral problems. Because of their Ne's penchant for breadth of ideation, an overly narrow focus can feel confining and uninteresting to INTPs. Exceptions to this may occur, however, when they feel they have stumbled onto a key insight into human behavior, such as Mihalyi Csikszentmihalyi's work on flow experiences.

Another potential hang-up for INTPs is the sentiment that social scientific findings do little more than confirm what is already obvious to intuition or common sense. One could see how this could hamper their motivation and cause them to see such work as unimportant or unnecessary. This might even prompt them to reconsider the hard sciences, whose results seem less knowable or obvious to common sense.

Because of their ambivalence toward formal research, INTPs often think twice before striving for academic tenure in any field. They may weigh the pros and cons of academic work versus freelancing or more applied sorts of work. Since we will discuss freelancing and the academic route below, we will discuss only the applied option here.

Unless approached in an entrepreneurial fashion, applied work can have some potential drawbacks for INTPs. One of these is dealing with red tape and various organizational rules. As we've seen, INTPs prefer to avoid functioning as employees if at all possible. Moreover, many types of applied work may seem too far removed from the conceptual realm, thereby making them less attractive to INTPs. Hence, the best type of applied work for INTPs would both inform and stimulate their conceptual interests.

Scholarship / Humanities

Scholarship, commonly associated with historical or humanities research, is another Investigative route for INTPs. Unsurprisingly, it too comes with a few potential drawbacks. Among these are the detailed nature of the work, its relative lack of "hard" or "eternal" truths, as well as what can seem like a lack of clear or immediate benefit to humanity (Fe).

Scholarship requires a great deal of patience and devotion to a single subject, which more impulsive INTPs often lack. It can also resemble certain scientific enterprises in its lack of clear import or application to human life. The idea of investing a great deal of time and effort into work that only a handful of other scholars will read can be difficult for INTPs to swallow.

This is not to say that scholarship isn't a great option for INTPs unconcerned with the applicability of their work. It is undoubtedly an excellent exercise and challenge for their Ti and Ne, providing a near infinite amount of material to wrestle with. Scholarship also has fewer Te demands than the sciences, allowing much of the exploration to occur in the conceptual realm, without concern for experimental procedures, research funding, etc. So in many respects, scholarship seems more conducive to INTPs' top two functions than the formal sciences.

Computer Science & Simulations

Prior to the information age, investigating problems relied heavily on observation, data collection, and painstaking analyses. With advancements in computer science and technology, we now have an array of new investigative options out our disposal. One of the more intriguing of these is computer simulation.

Computer simulations are used in the study of natural, as well as human phenomena, aiding our understanding of systems (e.g., weather systems) too complex for other types of analysis. Some thinkers believe that simulation is the ideal way to do science. In many cases, it is a cheaper and faster route. So instead of having to fund and conduct a laboratory experiment, one could simply program and run a computer simulation.

Simulation begins with developing a model that represents the problem or system being studied. After developing the model, the simulation is run to gain insight into the behavior of the system being studied. Simulations are often displayed via computer generated imagery, as is now commonplace in the analysis of weather patterns.

Computer simulation may captivate INTPs for a number of reasons. It involves a nice balance of analysis (e.g., identifying the basic laws or features of systems for model building), experimentation (e.g., "Let's tweak this variable and see what happens."), and interpretation ("What is this telling us?"), as well as the potential for generalization ("Is there a general principle here that might be true of other systems?"). While similar things could be said of the traditional sciences, simulation is attractive because it is often less tedious, less messy, and less costly than traditional experiments.

Some thinkers, such as philosopher David Chalmers, believe that using computers to simulate natural phenomena, such as evolution, may allow for, among other things, great advances in our understanding of intelligence. Philosopher Nick Bostrom, in his provocative

"Simulation Argument," suggests that intelligence acquired through simulation has huge implications for understanding ourselves (e.g., Are we living in a simulation?) and our future.

The capacity of artificial/computer-based intelligence to surpass human intelligence, which many thinkers believe will happen within the next century or so, may serve as a strong motivator for INTPs to work within, or at least keep tabs on, this field. Indeed, one might even argue that our highest R & D priority is to enhance our computational power which, in theory, might allow us to tackle a host of complex problems that extend beyond the reach of human intelligence.

Freelance Investigations

The hard sciences, social sciences, and scholarship all require attention to detail, the adoption of certain standardized methods and practices, and, in many cases, partnering with a scientific or academic establishment. In type speak, they all entail Te practices, which in many ways run against the grain of Ti. This is why many INTPs opt to function as freelancing, independent investigators.

Freelancing allows INTPs to work with what I like to call "gists." INTPs love discerning the gist of a given topic or argument, and then connecting that gist with other gists in a weblike fashion (Ne). They enjoy extracting and explaining the basic storyline running through a sea of ideas, as well as translating technical jargon into everyday language. This is why INTPs often end up functioning as "popularizers." In translating complex concepts into layman's terms, INTPs also satisfy their desire to help others (Fe).

Another potential upside of freelance investigation is its lack of rigid standards. Unlike those engaged in formal or academic research, freelancers aren't beholden to a hard set of rules or standards. It's not that freelancing is entirely devoid of standards, but only that its standards are more implicit and broadly distributed across its target audience. In this sense, freelancing can be seen as having Fe, rather than Te, sorts of standards. The notion that the truth or quality of one's work will reveal itself through a bottom-up, democratic (Fe) sort of process can be of great appeal to INTPs.

With that said, there are times when Fe endorsement may seem a bit flimsy or dubious to the rational-minded INTP. This may leave INTP freelancers feeling ungrounded, isolated, or uncertain about the actual quality or validity of their work. Freelancing also fails to offer the putative financial stability of working for a scientific or academic establishment.

* * *

Here is our list of potential INTP Investigative careers and majors:

- Biology, neuroscience

- Consciousness studies

- Computer science

- Health sciences

- Research assistant

- Social sciences (psychology, geography, history, sociology, political science)

- Scholar: history, humanities

- Nanotechnology

- Environmental science/studies

- Linguistics/semiotics, communication studies

- Philosophy, theology

- Population ethics, neuroethics, moral science

- Comparative religion

- Peace studies

- "People analytics"

- Information/library sciences

- Interdisciplinary studies

- Actuary

- Financial planning/investing

- Investigative journalist, reporter, freelancer

- Non-fiction author, writer, science writer

- Search engine optimization (SEO) expert/consultant

- Environmental law

Artistic (A)

If we roughly associate the Investigative domain with convergent thinking, we might pair the Artistic domain with divergent thinking. Typologically, the Artistic domain correlates with a preference for Intuition, as well as, to a lesser extent, Feeling and Perceiving. Artistics tend to perform especially well on the verbal portion of aptitude tests.

Artistics are highly represented among students studying the arts and humanities. Like those with Investigative-Artistic (IA) interests, individuals with Artistic-Investigative (AI) interests may gravitate toward the social sciences or interdisciplinary studies, which tend to involve a combination of creative and rational thinking.

INTPs might do well to conceive of themselves as artists, or at least subjectivists, because of the nature of their top two functions. But as dominant Thinkers, some INTPs may be reluctant to do so. Writing is among the more popular art forms among INTPs, serving as an excellent medium for exploring and developing their intellectual interests. More visually-inclined INTPs may gravitate toward architecture or web design, while more tech-savvy INTPs may take up work in fields like software design.

Here is our rather brief list of INTP Artistic careers:

- Graphic/web/software design

- Architecture

- Writer, blogger, Indy/self-publishing

Social (S)

Individuals in the Social interest domain enjoy working with people. They often prefer Feeling, as well as to some extent, Extraversion.

INTPs may take interest in Social careers because of the influence of their inferior Fe. As mentioned earlier, I generally discourage INTPs from choosing careers that routinely involve directly helping or advising people. If INTPs do opt to perform this type of work, they are usually wise to do it in smaller chunks, such as working part-time. On the whole, INTPs are better off influencing people in less direct ways, such as through Artistic or Investigative work.

Counseling / Psychology

We've seen how INTPs are interested in understanding human beings and how they might live better. It is therefore unsurprising that INTPs might consider psychotherapy as a potential career.

Psychotherapy is a helping profession. In many ways, it can also be viewed as an Fi profession, involving the investment of significant time and energy into a relatively small number of individuals. This is a rather formidable problem for INTPs, since, at least in theory, Fi is the very last function at their disposal; it is buried deep in their unconscious, even farther than Fe. Moreover, because of their Ti preference for self-help and self-sufficiency, INTPs can be rather impatient with those they perceive as weak, needy, irrational, or otherwise incapable of helping themselves.

In order for INTPs to enjoy their work as therapists, they need to find a way to keep the work stimulating and interesting. So instead of thinking of therapy in terms of the Fi individual, they may be better off reframing the psychotherapeutic context as a sort of laboratory for mutual learning and experimentation. Viewed this way, they might better appreciate and value the novel challenges of each client and, in turn, function as more effective therapists. Their interest in working with people-oriented (Fe) ideas (Ne) and strategies (Ti) may compensate for their relative lack of emotional empathy for the individual. Even then, INTP therapist would not be equipped to work with all types of clients. They may still have little patience, for instance, for those presenting as highly dysfunctional, neurotic, or otherwise "abnormal." Presumably due to their Ti-Fe pairing, INTPs are typically more interested in working with those with a more or less "normal" psychology. NTJs, by contrast, who use Te-Fi, often seem more interested in abnormal psychology and psychiatric disorders.

INTPs may also struggle to provide sound relational advice, since relationships do not come naturally or easily to them. They are typically more interested in individual therapy, often using a combination of meaning-centered, cognitive-behavioral, and mindbody techniques.

Career counseling may be the safest avenue for INTPs. It has the advantage of being less emotional and therefore less taxing on the INTP. INTPs also enjoy learning about various careers and knowledge areas, including trends (especially theoretical and methodological trends) within and among various disciplines. On the other hand, one can see how career counseling might become less interesting for

INTPs over time, as it provides fewer opportunities to probe deep into the psyche than other types of counseling.

In the end, I think it is reasonable to suggest that, in general, only the most psychoemotionally mature INTPs should consider working as psychotherapists. Even then, INTPs therapists are probably wise to limit themselves to part-time work, since dealing with others' emotions in an extraverted fashion can be extremely draining for INTPs.

College Teaching / Professorship

Becoming a college professor is a common dream among INTPs. The romance of being ensconced in a knowledge-centered environment can be of great appeal. For INTP geniuses, reality may approximate this romantic ideal. Such individuals may be relatively absolved from the extraneous duties associated with obtaining or maintaining academic tenure. For those with more mortal minds, however, academic life is rarely as idyllic as common romantic conceptions might suggest.

While there are several routes for working in academia, we will take a broad approach and discuss two main tracks. The first and most commonly envisioned track, involves becoming a tenured faculty member at a university. This is by far the more challenging of our two options, since it involves high competition for a relatively limited number of positions. The competition may be somewhat less fierce in some of the applied fields, such as health-related or applied science positions, since candidates often have additional career options (e.g., practicing as a nurse, attorney, engineer, etc.), many of which are more lucrative than the academic route.

In addition to fierce competition, becoming a tenured faculty member also requires considerable prerequisite legwork. This typically includes earning a doctorate level degree that includes a dissertation, as well as publishing ample original research ("publish or perish"). Requirements can be particularly stringent for "first-tier" schools, such as Harvard or Yale. Moreover, in many fields, research can be costly, thereby requiring researchers to constantly seek out and apply for grants. This is to say nothing of the teaching requirements, which can be quite hefty for non-tenured faculty. In short, the path to becoming a tenured faculty member, especially in the humanities or basic sciences, is in many ways like rushing for a fraternity, only that it involves doing so for many years, rather than just a few weeks.

Our second academic track is a less strenuous one, involving teaching at a community college or part-time at a university. This route entails few, if any, publishing requirements and positions are generally easier to come by. This is because these positions are focused less on research and more on teaching. Although INTPs who are fluid orators may enjoy the teaching element, most are drawn to the academy for its intellectual atmosphere and the opportunity to conduct research. Therefore, INTPs without the drive, intellect, or resilience to obtain a tenured position may view college teaching as a sort of "middle of the road" career option. They may opt to teach for the sake of paying the bills while using their free time to pursue their real passions.

* * *

Here is our list of potential INTP Social jobs and careers:

- Restaurant server/bartender (a decent "day job" for INTPs)

- College professor

- Counselor/psychologist(?)

Enterprising (E)

The Enterprising domain entails the promotion of products, ideas, or services. Enterprisers tend to be persuasive and assertive, enjoying competitive environments. Typical Enterprising careers include sales and marketing, business and management, politics, journalism, insurance, stock trading, and certain types of law. Enterprising individuals often prefer Extraversion.

Although INTPs are typically not drawn to Enterprising work for its own sake, they may, as we've seen, opt to pick up some business and marketing skills for the sake of entrepreneurship. If they combine such skills with some degree of technical savvy and ingenuity, INTPs can make a decent living through web-based or other sorts of enterprises.

Here is our extremely long list of INTP Enterprising careers and majors:

- Entrepreneur, web-based

- Consultant, web/software/IT

Conventional (C)

Individuals with Conventional interests enjoy administrative work. They are organized and detail-oriented, typically doing well with manipulating data. Those in this domain often prefer Sensing, Thinking, and/or Judging.

While typically not enjoying Conventional work, INTPs can typically perform it competently when necessary. But because this domain is rarely among their top interest areas, I have no Conventional careers or majors to recommend.

What About Medicine?

Medicine is a high-status career, as physicians are known and respected for their knowledge, intelligence, and impressive salaries. It is therefore unsurprising that INTPs might be curious about medical careers.

Medicine doesn't fit neatly into any of the Holland domains. Depending on the medical specialty, it involves some combination of I, R, and S interests. At least in the United States, medicine takes a heavily Te approach to human health, seeing many conditions in black-and-white terms. Ti and Ne, by contrast, tend to envision health along a continuum, which can make various diagnostic categorizations seem dubious and arbitrary to INTPs. Moreover, since INTPs' extraverted Judging function (Fe) is low in their functional stack, they may struggle to make firm diagnoses, which many patients expect in today's system. What is more, the drug and procedure-orientation of modern medicine runs counter to INTPs' bent toward more natural (Ne-Si) or self-help (Ti) approaches. INTPs see the body as well-equipped to heal itself and believe that people can in large part manage their own health. They therefore gravitate toward the prevention and self-care side of things.

For what it's worth, *The MBTI Manual* indicates that INTP med students are among the least enthusiastic in clinical settings, joined, unsurprisingly, by INFPs and ENTPs. Its posits that NPs' rugged individualism may be largely responsible for this finding.

INTPs who have already started medical school may find medical research the most promising avenue. Other potential specialties include psychiatry, behavioral medicine, and neurology. Psychiatry and behavioral medicine are the most obvious areas in which INTPs could regularly employ their Ti and Ne.

7. RELATIONSHIPS

INTPs need some measure of human contact. Few can live in complete isolation. Indeed, because of their Fe inferior, INTPs can be energized by having people around, even if not engaging with them directly. If cut off from people for too long, they may feel lonely or isolated.

As we've seen, engaging with people can give INTPs' Fe an ego boost. INTPs often hope to impress others with their charm, wit, and intellect. But when INTPs identify too strongly with what we might call their "public persona," thereby compromising their Ti selves, they can grow depressed and unsatisfied. Persistently sacrificing Ti for the sake of Fe is rarely beneficial to their personal growth or happiness.

What INTPs perceive as the "magical" qualities of Fe can make them giddy with dreams of love and romance, especially early in life. They may find themselves smitten by types exuding warmth and feeling, since these qualities are typically absent from the INTP's inner world. They may feel that pairing with a Feeling type nicely complements their Thinking and furthers their sense of psychological wholeness.

Pairing with a Feeler can also function like a sort of psychological insurance policy, preventing the INTP from swinging too far in the direction of Thinking. INTPs often lack confidence in their ability to successfully reconcile their T and F outside the context of a relationship. For some INTPs, this may indeed be a valid concern. Those early in their type development, for instance, may be more inclined to suffer from extreme or unstable thinking. For such individuals, a relationship may provide a sense of safety and stability, a set of training wheels if you will, which can aid their growth and development.

The problem with INTPs entering relationships for F reasons is that, once their F needs are satisfied, their focus naturally reverts to their T interests. When this occurs, they can easily get swept up in their T pursuits and completely lose contact with their feelings toward their partner. They may then begin to wonder if they really love (or loved) their partner, even questioning whether they want the relationship at all. In other words, they turn their Ti skepticism toward the relationship to evaluate whether it is useful or sensible.

Reasons & Justifications for Relationships

Introverts require less stimulation from the outside world than extraverts do. They look to themselves, to their own minds, for stimulation. Like other introverts, INTPs are typically good at entertaining themselves. But there are certain things they can't readily procure for themselves: sex, children, love, support, companionship, etc. Of these, having children is probably the least of the INTP's concerns, especially for INTP males. And while INTPs can certainly enjoy sex, it too usually takes a back seat to their other interests.

With regard to companionship, INTPs can experience a strong sense of kinship from reading the works of likeminded others. They derive great joy from following an author's line of reasoning and engaging with his or her ideas. One of the beautiful things about written works is they can be carefully selected to match the INTP's current concerns and interests. Books may do for INTPs' Ne what new sexual experiences might for STPs or music for Feeling types.

But what about love? More than anything, INTPs love wrestling with ideas and working on their own projects. As cold as it may sound, loving people is sort of an afterthought for INTPs. Indeed, INTPs often display a greater concern for humanity in general (Fe) than they do for particular individuals (Fi). This is consistent with type theory, which predicts that Fi is INTPs' least used and developed function (i.e., their eighth function).

What about the need to receive or be loved? As we've seen, one feature of INTPs' inferior Fe is a desire for external affirmation. This need for affirmation seems closely related to the need to be loved and validated. Therefore, "love" for INTPs, often involves a "need to be needed." Putting aside, for the moment, the question of whether this is a real need or merely an indicator of low self-worth, this need may be satisfied in a few different ways.

Perhaps the ideal way for INTPs to satisfy their ostensible need to be needed is through their work. Since INTPs tend to identify with and invest significant time and energy into their work, they want their work to be externally recognized and validated. When their work is validated, they feel useful and valuable.

Another way INTPs can feel needed is by being a provider. Unfortunately, they may come to resent the provider role if they feel dissatisfied with their line of work, which can put them in a bind. On the one hand, if they quit their job, they risk losing, among other things, their valued role as provider. On the other hand, if they fail to make the necessary career changes, they run the risk of becoming increasingly depressed, restless, and resentful. In short, they are faced with the dilemma of risking their Fe security for the sake of greater Ti satisfaction in their work.

Another issue related to the provider role is this question of whether INTPs feel needed for their Ti and Ne, which they see as their authentic selves, versus being needed for financial (S) or emotional (F) reasons, which represent their less authentic selves.

Friendships are another way INTPs can feel needed. Since friendships typically come with fewer SF duties and expectations, they can be an effective way for INTPs to feel valued for their true selves. But the same thing that is advantageous about friendships—their lack of formal commitment—can also be viewed as a disadvantage by INTPs. Without a formal commitment, INTPs may fear, rightly or not, that they will fail to maintain their friendships and thereby run the risk of isolating themselves.

Viewed from without, this all may seem a rather silly game. After all, if INTPs' goal is a selfish one (i.e., to feel needed), then recruiting others to help them in this regard might look a lot like "using them." But to be fair to INTPs, we should recognize that other types unwittingly use each other just as readily.

Further complicating INTPs' relational concerns is the issue of time. As Don Riso and Russ Hudson have appropriately observed in their account of the Enneagram Five, INTPs can be hoarders and misers of time. Their objective is to maximize time to themselves for exploring and developing their interests. So whenever another person enters their personal space, INTPs may worry over what might happen to their cherished time. If INTPs are happy in their careers, time may be a relative non-issue, since they will have plenty of time to satisfy their Ti and Ne at work. If not, however, they may come to see their partner as a potential threat to their time and freedom.

With all that said, what would seem an admirable reason for INTPs to participate in a relationship is out of genuine interest in their partner. This would typically involve a love for his or her mind and ideas, the type of partner David Keirsey has dubbed a "mindmate." Even then, however, INTPs may wonder if a relationship is really worth their time, considering all the foreseeable difficulties and complications it may bring.

In weighing relationship options, INTPs may consider less conventional possibilities, such as communal living or open relationships. These can be attractive to their Ne's penchant for novelty, as well as their Fe's attraction to a breadth of relationships. The notion of an open-ended relationship, without any hard commitments, may appeal to many INTPs, at least in theory. Somewhat paradoxically, however, the more openness and freedom INTPs experience in a relationship, the more likely they are to value and commit to a single partner.

The prospect of foregoing a romantic relationship, or at least a conventional romantic relationship, can be quite scary for INTPs. One of the scariest elements is having a lack of Fe continuity or stability in their lives. They may look around, see everyone getting married, and worry about never having a lifelong partner. Even INTPs who realize that most relationships revolve around fear, insecurity, and illusions may struggle to some extent. There is still a part of the INTP, even if less conscious, that embraces the idea of a long-term (Si) relationship (Fe).

At this point, it may be worth mentioning that there is no law stating that INTPs need to make a once-and-for-all decision about how they should approach relationships. Indeed, this would seem to go against their preferred position of openness. Nor is there anything suggesting that migrating in and out of relationships is necessarily a bad thing.

If INTPs are focused on engaging the top portion of their functional stack, they will not be devoting a lot of conscious time or energy to worrying about love or Fe security. Rather, they will be concentrating on their Ti-Ne work. If, in doing so, a good partner happens to meander into their world, they can cherish and celebrate whatever time they might have together. If not, they can work to satisfy their Fe needs in other ways, such as through friendships, reading, co-housing, discussion groups, etc.

Relationships as a Forum for Learning & Exploration

If we think a bit outside the box, we might view INTP relationships as having little, if anything, to do with love (at least in the traditional sense), and more to do with mutual exploration, sharing, struggling, and learning.

INTPs value and appreciate experiential truth. Since their Ne tends to lack much as far as conviction or discrimination, they use both reason (Ti) and experience (Si) to hone their perspectives. So if INTPs are truly interested in zeroing in on truth, they can benefit from including an experiential / empirical component in their epistemology. For INTP chemists, this might come from laboratory data. For INTPs interested in self-knowledge, human psychology, or moral development, relationships could serve as their laboratory for learning and experimentation.

Given a sufficiently open and willing partner, there is really no limit to the sorts of experiments INTPs might conduct in their relationships. They might, for instance, entertain or trial less conventional practices, such as intentionally restricting various activities (e.g., conversations, sexual encounters, etc.) so as to heighten the level of interest when they do partake in them. Or, they might consider having separate living quarters, or even separate homes, to increase the sense of freedom and intensity in the relationship.

While creativity and experimentation can certainly make relationships more interesting for INTPs, even more foundational to their relational success are openness and honesty, or what I will call the "O & H policy."

The Openness & Honesty ("O & H") Policy

The O & H policy can be summarized as follows:

> Both partners will, to the best of their ability, be open and honest in their communication, especially with regard to their **negative** thoughts, feelings, experiences, concerns, and fears. This is to be the case regardless of how such communication is anticipated to be received by one's partner (i.e., in a positive or negative way).

The O & H policy is critical for several reasons. First, it helps INTPs value and feel close to their partners. If INTPs' partners can demonstrate their love and devotion through even the most difficult discussions, INTPs will increasingly come to value and respect them. INTPs cherish the rarity and maturity of a partner who is willing to courageously confront and deal with harsh or painful realities, as well as one who can love and accept the INTP for who he or she is—the good, bad, and the ugly.

If O & H relationships are anything, they are *real*. Real love must be founded on truth, even when it hurts. When partners are completely open and honest with each other, the roots of the relationship grow ever deeper as their problems, fears, and frustrations are successfully expressed, analyzed, and integrated.

Whenever INTPs fail to adhere to the O & H policy and fail to express their thoughts, they put the course of the relationship in grave danger. This is true for at least two reasons. First, the moment INTPs stop sharing certain thoughts with their partners is the moment they begin to detach from and devalue them. At that moment, the INTP is no longer relating to his or her partner, but has chosen to become a free agent.

Second, when INTPs fail to share their thoughts, the relationship immediately becomes less interesting to them. Remember, the most honest and authentic reason for INTPs to be in a relationship is to learn and explore with their partner. So as soon as they turn down an independent path and start moving away from their partner, they have forsaken the primary purpose of the relationship.

The Danger of Concealing Negative Thoughts & Assumptions

INTPs harbor a zillion thoughts and assumptions about relationships in general, as well as about themselves and their partners. But the vast majority of these thoughts are never shared or discussed, leading INTPs to function according to mental rules and assumptions of which their partners are relatively unaware. Even in the midst of conversations, INTPs formulate judgments they hesitate to release from the safe haven of their minds. Unfortunately, when INTPs conceal concerns about their partner or state of the relationship, they do neither themselves nor the relationship any favors.

Here are some examples of negative thoughts or assumptions INTPs may fail to share with their partners:

- "I don't think she really knows or loves me for who I am. She only loves an idealized image of me."

- "There she goes being irrational again. Another emotional rant."

- "I'm really not interested in what he is saying right now, I wish I could escape and do something else."

- "She is so needy and demanding. I wish she would just leave me be for a while."

- "I don't think this is the right relationship for me. I need to work on finding a way out."

- "I can only give him about an hour per day. The rest of the time I need for my work."

- "Since I agreed to this marriage, I guess I'm obligated to do x, y, and z."

In these instances, INTPs may carry on like everything is fine, giving their partners little indication they are having such thoughts. They adapt outwardly, while growing inwardly distant from their partners. This may even occur without the INTP being fully aware of it.

When INTPs fail to share their negative thoughts, they also prematurely close themselves to further information. For instance, by assuming their partner's emotional expressions are irrational, they prematurely rule out the possibility of there being a rational basis for such expressions, even if it is not immediately evident. By automatically assuming their subjective appraisals of their partners are correct, without seeking further information or clarification, INTPs are clearly in the wrong, acting pridefully, tyrannically, and egocentrically.

Finally, unshared thoughts and assumptions can lay the foundation for an alternate reality to which the INTP's partner has no access. As this alternate reality grows, it becomes increasingly difficult for INTPs to truly love their partners or to perceive them fairly and accurately.

INTP Communication Issues

We've already seen how INTPs may fail to express their thoughts or concerns out of fear of hurting their partner's feelings. Considering their status as Thinking types, this seems a bit strange, which suggests there may be more going on here than meets the eye.

In reality, INTPs may be less worried about their partner's feelings than they are about their own discomfort with navigating emotional situations. So by failing to be honest and direct in their communication, INTPs aren't really protecting their partners as much as they are protecting themselves; they aren't acting heroically, but cowardly.

INTPs may also fail to express their relational concerns for fear of saying something that will jeopardize the relationship (e.g., "If I tell her how I really feel, will she still love me or want to be with me?"). This is typically rooted in deeper fears, such as the fear of being alone, rejected, unloved, or unneeded.

Because their Fe is inferior, INTPs may also gravitate toward less direct means of self-expression. They may, for instance, enlist their Ne to make a point by way of questions. So instead of saying, "I think we should try X, Y, and Z in our relationship" they might say, "What do you think about couples who do X, Y, and Z in their relationship?" Or, rather than asserting "I'm tired of talking" they might ask their partner, "Are you feeling tired?"

INTPs may also self-express through actions rather than words. So instead of expressing their love or apologies verbally, they may do so through thoughtful acts or gestures. A less healthy form of indirect expression is passive-aggressive behavior. Passive-aggressiveness (P-A) involves the expression of frustration in indirect and underhanded ways. So rather than dealing directly with a relational grievance, INTPs might, for example, intentionally stay late at the office as a passive act of rebellion.

Improving Communication

As with other IP types, it is important for INTPs to understand that relational harmony should not be equated with relational health. While external harmony is often part of a healthy relationship, it really has little to do with genuine intimacy or effective communication.

In reality, developing genuine intimacy can be quite painful and difficult, requiring frequent confrontations the fears, insecurities, and ego/inferior function issues of both parties. When couples are working through these issues, moments of disharmony are all but inevitable.

Since intimate relationships are built on openness and honesty, they would ideally implement the O & H policy from the outset, thereby eliminating the need for years of untangling relational knots in therapy. The O & H policy may also reduce the total amount of pain, guilt, and shame accrued in a relationship.

In working to become more O & H, INTPs need to become more aware of when they are acting out of fear, which, as we've seen, typically involves their Fe sensitivities or insecurities. They must also recognize when they are failing to tell the whole truth. They can learn to catch themselves in situations where they might habitually avoid open and honest communication.

The "I will be okay" principle, which I introduced earlier, can provide a point of confidence for INTPs as they go about stretching themselves in the direction of unmitigated O & H. It is particularly important for INTPs to know that they can be okay without the relationship. This is in no way intended to diminish the value of the relationship nor the INTP's investment in it. But if INTPs feel their health and well-being is dependent on the relationship, they will be more likely to act out of fear and thereby fail to be O & H.

Working to recognize and understand one's inferior function issues, as well as those of one's partner, is also critical to effective communication. When an issue can be objectively identified as an "inferior function issue," it becomes much easier for partners to be mutually empathetic, as they remind themselves of the difficulty of dealing with their own inferior function issues.

Identity Issues: Lone Wolf (Ti) vs. Mr. Nice Guy (Fe)

The way INTPs approach and function in relationships directly relates to the degree to which they identify with their Ti versus Fe. As we've seen, INTPs may use Ne-Fe displays of wit, charm, and affability to ingratiate themselves to others. When dating, for instance, their affability may lead prospective partners to see them as thoughtful, sincere, and endearing. Some INTPs may even identify with these qualities, seeing themselves as "nice guys" (or gals) who can effortlessly get along with, or at least adapt to, nearly anyone.

The problem is that INTPs are not nearly as nice as the nice guy persona suggests. Their extraverted side is more of a social façade than a true representation of their inner selves. It therefore seems appropriate that INTPs, as well as their partners, take an honest look at who the INTP really is (and is not). Generally speaking, INTPs are not social butterflies with strong interests in the lives of others. They are more like lone wolves, fiercely independent and absorbed in their own thoughts and affairs.

In many cases, INTPs' "lone wolf" side may not fully manifest until well into the relationship. And when it finally does, partners may be taken aback by the INTP's fierce independence. They may even find themselves wondering which person—the nice guy or the lone wolf—is the real INTP. Those who fell in love with the nice guy INTP often revolt against the lone wolf, hoping the nice guy will soon regain control. They may use a variety of tactics—guilt, shame, pleading, etc.—to facilitate this process. In some cases, these tactics may work, at least in the short term, since many INTPs really want to retain the nice guy as part of their identity.

Unfortunately, what INTPs and their partners may fail to realize is that as long as the lone wolf is repressed or "caged," the INTP can never be an authentic partner. Moreover, it is only a matter of time before their repressed wolf will reemerge in a state of rebellion.

As lone wolves, INTPs need and desire a great deal of freedom and control. This can be further enumerated as follows:

- INTPs want to be in full control of themselves.

- They don't want to be responsible for controlling others.

- They don't want others to control them.

In light of INTPs' need for freedom and control, their partners are left with some tough decisions. Assuming they are committed to the relationship, their partners must discern the degree of freedom and autonomy they are willing to concede to the INTP. Many partners are reluctant to grant them complete freedom, which can often seem too scary. Instead, they may use various tactics, even unwittingly, to curtail or discourage the INTP's freedom. This back-and-forth game of Ti freedom versus Fe compliance may go on for years, or even a lifetime.

While it would be silly and unfair to suggest that partners should merely acquiesce to the INTP's every whim and wish, it is pretty much a guarantee that INTPs will be better partners when bestowed with ample Ti freedom. If endowed with the freedom to love and participate in the relationship on their own terms, they are more apt to engage with genuine interest and respect. This is the paradox of pairing with INTPs. Namely, the more one avoids the temptation to reign them in or make them feel guilty, the more the INTP will love and commit to the relationship.

Freedom to Doubt

Seasons of doubt and skepticism are part and parcel of being an INTP. This includes doubting and questioning their relationships. And because Fe is their inferior function, they can unfortunately be prone to losing faith and confidence in their relationships rather quickly. They may worry that each new relational problem or obstacle is irremediable, a portent of relational doom.

INTPs are especially prone to doubt their relationships when their partners express criticism or negative emotions toward them. For instance, they may misinterpret their partner's desire to discuss the relationship as a sign of personal failure or rejection. We might think of this in terms of Fe moping or insecurity.

While it is true that INTPs must develop greater faith in themselves and their partner with respect to handling relational problems, their partners must find a way to be okay with INTPs expressing their doubts and concerns about the relationship. For INTPs to remain fully committed to and invested in the relationship, there are times when they must review the reasons and rationale for the relationship. Of course, this can be extremely difficult and scary for most partners.

Feeling types, in particular, may fail to see why INTPs cannot simply rely on feelings to stay connected. They may struggle to see how the elusive nature of INTPs' feelings may cause them to lose sight of why they are in the relationship.

It can also be beneficial for INTPs and their partners to periodically review the INTP's Ti reasons for being in the relationship. This might include, for instance, highlighting the value of the relationship with respect to mutual learning and exploration.

If partners can grant INTPs the freedom to doubt, they have a far greater chance of earning the INTP's trust and respect. This can also serve as part of the Ti rationale for the relationship. With each new problem or obstacle that INTPs surmount with their partner, they develop a deeper sense of appreciation for and commitment to the relationship.

Attitudes toward Family & Parenting

We've already seen how INTPs can gravitate to a rather simple or Bohemian lifestyle. Since they don't have Extraverted Sensing (Se) in their functional stack, they are less concerned with aesthetics or material comforts than other types might be. And while INTPs might like the idea of making a good income, money is less important to them than pursuing their interests.

For those partnering with an INTP, this may translate into a sort of financial rollercoaster. Thus, individuals seeking a consistent financial provider may be better off pairing with another personality type. This is not to say that INTPs don't have the potential to make a solid or consistent income, but only that it should not be taken as a given.

With regard to children, INTPs aren't naturally "kid people." INTPs tend to be inwardly serious and focused on their own interests. My guess is that many INTPs (especially INTP males) merely defer to their partners with regard to having children, rather than acting on a strong personal interest. This is not to say that INTPs cannot or do not love their children, but only that raising children is rarely among their top priorities in life.

Unless asked to independently care for multiple children for extended periods of time, INTPs are generally good at modeling patience and temperance as parents. They tend to be more permissive than authoritarian, working to avoid compromising their child's freedom, uniqueness, or expressiveness. In other words, they tend to treat their children like they would want to be treated.

While not naturally playful, INTPs can enjoy limited periods of engagement with children. They may, however, feel torn between work and "family time," the latter of which can at times feel a bit dull. In many cases, spouses may feel the INTP is failing to invest adequately in this regard and may try to persuade them to do more. This, of course, can open the door to conflict if the INTP feels his autonomy is being compromised.

Final Thoughts

Because of the challenges associated with their Fe inferior, relational success can seem like an uphill battle for INTPs. As I've repeatedly asserted, vocational satisfaction seems an important precursor to INTPs' relational success. If still in career-development mode, they may fail to invest the necessary time and energy into their relationships. With that said, relationships can be an enriching and rewarding part of life for INTPs. Through open and honest discussions with their partners, they can learn a lot about life and about themselves.

8. COMPATIBILITY WITH OTHER TYPES

INTPs can get along with a variety of types. But their ability to blend with someone on a surface level should not be conflated with long-term compatibility potential. INTPs should also avoid granting their emotions too much weight when assessing compatibility. As we've seen, INTPs can be prime targets for being unconsciously wooed or manipulated by Feeling types. It is therefore important that INTPs give Ti the upper hand in selecting a long-term partner. This of course flies in the face of conventional wisdom, which suggests that everyone should just "listen to their heart."

For long-term compatibility, INTPs need a partner who allows them to functional authentically as INTPs, including granting them sufficient freedom of action and expression. They seek a partner with similar intellectual interests and capacities, or what David Keirsey has called a "mindmate."

When paired with a mindmate, INTPs feel that, at any given moment, there is potential for a meaningful exploration of ideas with their partner. INTPs may be especially drawn to those with knowledge and interests overlapping with their own, making way for a sort of co-exploration of truth. Ideally, the INTP's mindmate would also be open to adopting the O & H policy. Such a partner would typically be rather open-minded, with enough maturity and self-worth to handle the inherent difficulties of an O & H relationship. Typically, such a mate will come in the form of another Intuitive type.

Lifestyle is another important compatibility consideration for INTPs. While INTPs can be quite flexible when it comes to living arrangements, they may worry that a relationship may increase their financial burden. Since many INTPs dream of having more time to pursue their personal interests, they tend to seek partners who are either financially independent or are content with a rather simple lifestyle. INTPs may come to resent partners that expect them to work undesirable jobs or longer hours just to have nicer stuff.

With that said, we will now explore INTPs' potential compatibility with various personality types.

INTP-ENFJ Pairings

INTPs and ENFJs are similar in that both utilize a dominant Judging function. This contributes to a shared tendency to be intentional, proactive, and goal-oriented. These types also share the Ti-Fe function pair, which, combined with their shared preference for Intuition, may contribute a similarity of interests and worldview.

These types also differ in some important ways. Perhaps most important is the fact their Ti and Fe functions fall at opposite ends of the functional stack. While this may engender a fierce initial attraction a la the "opposites attract" principle, once the infatuation has waned, it may contribute to a number of difficulties.

ENFJs have strong personalities. Their Fe assertions can be direct, intense, and emotionally-charged. Such judgments, especially when unsolicited, are not always well received by others, especially by independent-minded INTPs.

ENFJs are also prone to function like teachers and counselors in their relationships. They love sharing their insights in order to help their partners grow and self-actualize. They enjoy having problems to solve and people to help. Consequently, their romantic relationships commonly take on a teacher-pupil (or parent-child) sort of pattern. In fact, any relationship comprised of a J-type and P-type would seem to carry this potential.

At least for a while, INTPs may like the fact that ENFJs can help them learn about relationships in general and themselves in particular. As long as the relationship serves as a platform for learning, INTPs are likely to stay interested, while tolerating or overlooking what they might otherwise view as less favorable features of the ENFJ. Not surprisingly, these less favorable features often pertain to the ENFJ's Fe.

Although INTPs may love the ENFJ's Fe when it helps them learn about themselves, they may start to feel differently if they feel the ENFJ no longer has anything new or valuable to say. Indeed, once the initial novelty has worn off, INTPs may grow cold or resentful toward the ENFJ's hair-trigger Fe. As we've seen, INTPs instinctively eschew or resist those they perceive as trying to control or manage them. So while they may enjoy, or at least tolerate, being the ENFJ's pupil for a while, if the ENFJ continues trying to teach or criticize them when they are no longer interested, they will eventually rebel and things will get ugly.

INTPs may also struggle with ENFJs' loquaciousness and tendency toward emotionality and melodrama. Since ENFJs "feel aloud," INTPs may find themselves looking for a quiet place where they can be alone with their own thoughts. They may feel they can never relax and fall into Ti mode when their ENFJ partner is around. Accordingly, the ENFJ may complain about the INTP being too detached, aloof, or emotionally checked-out.

Lifestyle can be another point of contention between these two types. ENFJs often have refined tastes with regard to their material surroundings, their physical appearance, as well as their palate. Like

INFJs, they commonly display a taste for the finer things in life—fine arts, food, music, culture, etc. They may at times be perceived as snobbish or uppity (think of the sitcom character, Frasier Crane, for example), taking themselves or their sophisticated tastes a bit too seriously. As we've seen, INTPs are exactly the opposite in this respect, gravitating toward a lifestyle of earthiness and minimalism.

In light of the above, it seems fairly unlikely that INTPs would enjoy long-term compatibility with ENFJs, at least not without great struggle. To be successful, both partners would need to be far along in their personal growth and development, in which case an ENFJ might serve as a suitable mindmate and O & H partner for the INTP.

INTP-ENTJ Pairings

Since both are dominant Thinking types, INTPs and ENTJs are bound to have some things in common. Both can be ambitious, for instance, although in somewhat different ways. ENTJs' ambition will tend toward practical matters, such as a heading up a company or enterprise. By contrast, INTPs' ambitions are often more abstract than practical, involving the development and refinement of concepts rather than tactics or logistics.

Similar to what we saw with ENFJs, ENTJs often assume the role of teacher or leader in the relationship. In many ways, ENTJs cannot help but take the lead in whatever circumstance they find themselves. The problem, of course, is that INTPs are typically less than enthusiastic about being led. They are their own leaders, instinctively rebelling against external coercion. Therefore, establishing parity and mutual respect is likely to be one of the foremost challenges for this type pairing.

One potential benefit of pairing with ENTJs is they tend to be financially successful. This could be a boon for INTPs if it had the effect of relieving some of their financial strains. And since ENTJs often enjoy the role of provider, such an arrangement could feasibly work out quite nicely.

A potential drawback might involve the ENTJ having little interest in introspection or self-awareness. If the ENTJ were to be too consumed with the extraverted application of T and N, such as in business and enterprise, the INTP may feel they have little in common.

On the whole, if an INTP-ENTJ duo can get beyond the initial power struggle and avoid falling into teacher-pupil roles (which may be no small task), this pairing would seem to have ample potential for success.

INTP-ENFP Pairings

INTPs and ENFPs can bond in the world of Ne. Both types enjoy absorbing and connecting circulating ideas and concepts. Both are open to unconventional ideas, values, and lifestyles, although some ENFPs (like ENTPs) may be less open than expected due to the pull of their inferior Si.

INTPs can be drawn to the Bohemian, peripatetic ways of ENFPs. Like INTPs, ENFPs are seekers. The primary difference is that ENFPs are more apt to physically function as seekers, wanderers, and travelers than INTPs are. ENFPs enjoy travelling and experiencing different cultures. While INTPs may be a bit less inclined or adventurous in this regard, they may nonetheless appreciate the ENFP's openness and free-spiritedness.

A potential drawback of this pairing is that some ENFPs may lack sufficient depth of thought or focus for the INTP's taste. While INTPs certainly enjoy exploring a breadth of topics, there are also times when they want to talk in greater depth about a particular issue. If the ENFP seems incapable of going deeper or sustaining concentration, the INTP may lose faith in her potential as a suitable mindmate.

Despite their shared Ne, these types may also struggle with differences in interests and worldview. ENFPs are often interested in arts, culture, languages, and children. When it comes to psychology, they often take a cultural or nuture-based perspective. INTPs, by contrast, tend to be more interested in philosophy and gravitate toward the nature side of psychological issues. So even when INTPs and ENFPs are interested in similar subjects (e.g., psychology), they may find themselves taking different approaches or arriving at different conclusions. This is not to say that differences or disagreements are necessarily a bad thing, but there is something to be said for being on the same page with regard to values, beliefs, and worldview.

In short, INTPs and ENFPs often share much in common, at least on the surface. With further engagement, however, they may find their values and worldview are too different to warrant a continuance of the relationship, especially if involving disagreements over having children. Therefore, while some INTP-ENFP pairings may work quite well, others may fizzle out rather quickly.

INTP-ENTP Pairings

INTPs are likely to find better compatibility with ENTPs than ENFPs. This is due to the fact that ENTPs use all the same functions as INTPs, only in a slightly different order.

Despite the E-I difference, these two types tend to think along surprisingly similar lines, capable of finding common ground on a broad range of subjects. As with ENFPs, however, ENTPs can be prone to hold tightly to certain traditions or religious worldviews that fail to resonate with the INTP. This is not always a deal breaker, however, since these types typically have enough in common to surmount ideological differences.

These types may also enjoy some measure of compatibility in their lifestyle preferences. While ENTPs may be a bit more worldly in terms of their material wants, this pairing can typically find common ground in the financial arena. With that said, ENTPs are more socially inclined than INTPs. Many enjoy children and want a good-sized family. Like other extraverts, they enjoy being busy and are undeterred by constant activity and commotion. Therefore, disagreements over family life could prove a potential sticking point for these types.

In short, the INTP-ENTP pairing has good potential for relational success, as these types can enjoy great intellectual kinship and camaraderie. Differences with respect to children and family may serve as the primary impediments to an otherwise natural compatibility.

INTP-INFJ Pairings

Having examined this type pairing in significant depth on Personality Junkie, we will content ourselves with a less extensive account here.

Despite their general love of people, INFJs may struggle when it comes to finding a worthy and compatible romantic partner. They feel frustrated when others fail to see and appreciate them for their deeper Ni selves. While others may affirm and appreciate their Fe warmth and personableness, it is Ni, not Fe, that serves as the nucleus of the INFJ's identity. For this reason, INFJs seek a partner who values and understands them on a deeper metaphysical level.

Early in the relationship, INTPs may be particularly skeptical toward the workings and outpourings of the INFJ's Ni and Fe. While INTPs trust their own Ti logic, Ni can seem a rather foreign, even if intriguing, epistemological tool. Whereas Ti tends to think in binary terms (i.e., "It is either this or it is that."), Ni seems more at home with paradox (i.e., "There is a way it can be *both* this and that.").

Ni can also seem a bit overreaching or unempirical for INTPs' taste. For this reason, INTPs may find better luck with INFJs who have grown into their tertiary Ti, allowing INFJs to connect their intuitions with existing concepts, frameworks, or taxonomies.

INTPs who remain patient and open to the possibility of Ni being a powerful tool for apprehending truth can eventually see and appreciate its inherent value. In the INFJ, INTPs can find a wellspring of psychological perceptiveness, birthing insights they, in lacking Ni, may fail to achieve on their own. INTPs love the fact that INFJs can see things that they, despite much introspection, have remained essentially blinded to. INFJs' insights can serve to expedite INTPs' personal development, as well as their understanding of human nature.

The unique way that Ni perceives the world can serve as a consistent point of attraction for INTPs. This is one reason why INTPs and INFJs can make wonderful companions. The INTP values the INFJ's originality and perceptiveness, while the INFJ loves the fact that the INTP wants to metaphysically commune with her. It can be an utter delight and great relief when INFJs, notoriously misunderstood and underappreciated, discover that one of the most logical and intellectual personality types finds their insights both valuable and interesting.

With that said, INFJs may struggle with the INTP's relative dearth of Fe emotional expressiveness. This is especially evident in emotional or romantic situations where INTPs fail to display what the INFJ considers the appropriate type or degree of feeling or expressiveness.

Like other types, INFJs may also struggle with INTPs' fierce need for independence. They may also become frustrated with INTPs' tendency to be distant or distracted, with their inability to remain consistently focused or present in a discussion. More than anything else, INFJs value long and in-depth conversations with their partners. So when INTPs seem restless or disinterested, the INFJ will eventually become frustrated.

INTPs and INFJs also use different Sensing functions (INTPs use Si, INFJs use Se), which can roughly be associated with lifestyle preferences. As Se types, INFJs tend to be more liberal in their expenditures, especially when it comes to what they consider "high quality" goods or experiences. Like their ENFJ counterparts, INFJs tend to develop refined and cultured tastes, or what the IN ᴊ . _ deem "expensive" tastes. INTPs operate at the opposite end of the spectrum, opting for more Spartan living conditions and less refined tastes (with the possible exception of good coffee!). INTPs are more interested in refining their logic and theories than their SF tastes. These differences may serve as points of contention for these types, although are typically not deal breakers should the couple align in other ways.

Similar to what we saw with ENFJs, INTPs may also struggle with INFJs' strong and frequent Fe judgments, as well as their tendency toward emotionality and melodrama. Emotionally young INTPs, in particular, may struggle with what at times may seem like a steady stream of criticism flowing from the INFJ. Consequently, the INFJ may fail to satisfy INTPs' desire for Fe affirmation, or their "need to be needed." What such INTPs may fail to recognize, however, is that the INFJ's critiques may actually help them move beyond their unhealthy Fe habits. After all, as long as INTPs are relying on others for affirmation, they can never truly be free. This is not to say that INFJs are never off target or excessive in their criticisms, nor that they should never praise or affirm the INTP. The key is to find the right balance, allowing both partners to function healthily and authentically.

On the whole, INFJs are probably one of the best matches for INTPs. Their interests are often quite similar and they tend to complement each other nicely. Their shared introversion allows both to feel at ease with a quieter, slower-paced lifestyle. INFJs can also serve as excellent exemplars of the O & H policy, since they are naturally inclined to openly express what they are feeling. While INTPs may initially find the INFJ's Fe pronouncements difficult to handle, they can come to recognize their value in developing a healthy, O & H relationship.

INTP-INTJ Pairings

Since INTJs do not extravert Feeling, INTPs are not energetically drawn to them in the way they are to certain F types. Especially on first encounter, INTJs may seem too cold and unfriendly for the INTP's more neighborly Fe. But as we've seen, it is not advisable for INTPs to judge prospective partners by way of feeling. Hence, pairing with an INTJ should not be prematurely ruled out based on initial impressions.

As with INFJs, INTPs can find much to value in INTJs' Ni. They may be impressed and inspired by its ability to penetrate deeply and perspicaciously into various topics. And since INTJs are predominantly Perceivers (Ni), they often pick up on things that INTPs miss. Hence, INTJs can make fascinating conversation partners for INTPs. These two types may be especially compatible if they share similar interests, which is often the case.

With that said, INTJs can be terse and brutally honest. As with other J-types, it can take time for INTPs to acclimate to their stark directness. In time, however, INTPs can come to appreciate, even aspire to, such directness of expression. After all, if INTPs are seeking a relationship founded on openness and honesty, why not pair with a J-type who already exemplifies these virtues?

Another potential benefit of pairing with INTJs is they may be relatively uninterested in having multiple children. This makes it easier for INTPs to focus on their work, while also freeing up more time for the relationship.

In short, although INTPs and INTJs are not prone to "love at first sight," they can often enjoy good compatibility through shared interests, stimulating dialogue, and honest communication.

INTP-INFP Pairings

INFPs are among the more common of the Intuitive types. They can readily be found lingering in (or working at) coffee shops and bookstores around the world.

While INFPs with a strong Ne can be attractive to INTPs, the sense of initial attraction between these two types is typically modest at best. INFPs are less apt to embellish their appearance (e.g., to use make-up or other adornments) than FJ or SFP types, which, for better or worse, may influence the INTP's initial impression of them. Their lack of external warmth may also fail to impress or inspire the INTP's Fe. But again, it is generally unwise for INTPs to put much stock in their first impressions.

A more serious concern for this pairing is many INFPs, especially INFP females, see having children as one of their primary objectives in life. A deep love of children (especially their own) is one of the more common features of Fi types. Consequently, many INFPs are looking for a reliable provider and family-oriented individual, which, as we've seen, is typically not one of the INTP's most authentic priorities.

With that said, INTPs do have potential for compatibility with some INFPs, particularly those who are highly intelligent and idea-oriented. These types are also likely to enjoy strong compatibility with respect to lifestyle preferences. Both have minimalist and Bohemian tendencies, content to live with less rather than more. Both types also enjoy reading and exchanging ideas a la Ne.

There may be some clashes, however, when the INTP's Ti steps on the INFP's Fi toes, causing the INFP to feel hurt or offended. Even more importantly, this may have the effect of dissuading the INTP from being open and honest, which may already prove difficult in a relationship comprised of two IP types, who are less communicative by nature.

IP pairings who fail to be O & H may find themselves entrenched in a passive-aggressive power struggle. Since INTPs and INFPs are both inner J-types, they can be stubborn and insist on their own way of doing things. And without effective communication, they may end up doing their own thing without really developing the relationship.

This seems less likely when INPs are paired with J-types or, to some extent, with E-types.

In short, the relative incompatibility of Fi and Ti, as well as foreseeable communication issues, makes the INFP-INTP pairing a precarious one. This is not to say that two highly developed INPs could not enjoy good compatibility, but a lot of things would have to fortuitously come together for such a relationship to thrive.

INTP-INTP Pairings

As with INTP-INFP pairings, INTP couples can be plagued by communication issues. Unlike INFP-INTP couples, however, they aren't forced to contend with Fi-Ti differences. The fact that two INTPs share all the same functions can help them naturally read and understand each other. This may be a plus in the sense of being able to empathize with and forgive each other. But it might also detract from the level of interest and intrigue that comes from type differences.

On the whole though, I think INTP-INTP pairings have good potential for success. INTP couples can define their relationship however they want, without concern for tradition or convention. They can encourage each other to be their most authentic selves, figuring out, together, what the "good life" might look like for INTPs.

Pairing with Sensing Types

The reason I'm lumping the Sensing types together is I generally feel INTPs are better off pairing with another Intuitive type. As David Keirsey points out, similarity in the S-N domain seems especially beneficial. In my experience, a shared N preference is particularly important for INTPs.

With that said, it is not at all uncommon for INTPs to pair with SP types. This is due, at least in part, to the fact that SPs are extremely common, especially in the United States. SPs are action-oriented, your proverbial "doers." This is especially true of ESPs, who are the most hands-on and active of all types.

INTPs often find ESPs physically attractive, while also being drawn to their spontaneous and fun-loving demeanor. Unfortunately, because of their inferior N, ESPs often fail to satisfy the INTP's mindmate criteria.

ISPs can also be quite physically active and attractive, with the added benefit of being somewhat more reflective than ESPs. Unfortunately, INTPs may struggle with similar communication issues (or perhaps even worse) with ISPs as they do with INPs. Moreover, with the exception of certain highly intelligent ISPs, most ISPs will prove unsatisfactory mindmates for INTPs. This makes it difficult to recommend SPs, in general, as good potential matches for INTPs.

When it comes to STJs, INTPs are unlikely to find much as far as initial or ultimate compatibility. SFJs, however, have this magical function called Fe, which can readily tug on the INTP's unconscious heart strings. The magical powers of Fe may be particularly prominent in ESFJs, who use Fe as their dominant function. Unfortunately, INTPs and ESFJs are likely to encounter some of the same problems as INTP-ENFJ pairings. Among other things, the strength and frequency of the ESFJ's extraverted judgments may be off-putting to the INTP, while the INTP's lack of Fe expressiveness may leave the ESFJ wanting. And like other S types, ESFJs, unless highly intelligent, may fail to satisfy the INTP's mindmate requirements.

ISFJs may be more authentically appealing to INTPs because they tend to be more reflective than ESFJs. Like ESFJs, they also have all the same functions as INTPs, only in a different order. Although their N function is inferior, this may be compensated for, at least to some degree, by their introversion. I have known several ISFJs, especially ISFJ males, who enjoy fairly abstract discussions. And because they share all the INTP's functions, they may enjoy discussing similar subjects. Whether a given ISFJ will prove a worthy mindmate for INTPs is hard to predict. It is also difficult to predict how the ISFJ might handle the INTP's forays into unconventional, dark, or nihilistic territories. If the ISFJ proves capable of meeting these criteria, he or she may in fact prove a worthy partner for the INTP. We might therefore conclude that, of all the Sensing types, INTPs might have the best chance of long-term success with ISFJs, with ISTPs serving as a likely runner-up.

9. DISTINGUISHING INTPS FROM RELATED TYPES

At first blush, determining one's personality type might seem fairly simple and straightforward. But for many folks, especially INP types, this is not the case. Many labor for months, even years, before feeling confident in their type designation.

The reasons people struggle to identify their type are manifold. Lack of self-knowledge is a major factor, as is deficient understanding of the types. Another challenge is the paradoxical nature of the psyche itself, the fact that each personality type is comprised of two pairs of opposing functions. And because the psyche desperately wants to feel whole, the less conscious functions may unduly influence questionnaire responses, leading Feelers to test as Thinkers, Sensors as Intuitives, and so on.

Further complicating matters is the individual's level of personal growth. As we get older (so the theory goes) we develop our weaker functions and things begin to balance out. This is why typing at a younger age may in some ways be more accurate than doing so in adulthood. It's worth remembering, however, that growth and maturity does not change our basic type. While personal growth may make it trickier to discern our actual preferences, the essential structure of our type is immutable.

The purpose of this chapter is to highlight and clarify some of the common differences between INTPs and related personality types— ENTPs, ISTPs, INFPs, and INTJs. We will begin by comparing and contrasting INTPs with their ENTP counterparts.

INTP vs. ENTP

ENTPs' functional stack is as follows: Ne-Ti-Fe-Si. From this we learn that ENTPs use all the same functions as INTPs, only in a slightly different order. Consequently, they may appear quite similar in both their presentation and ideation. Upon closer examination, however, it is possible to identify some noteworthy differences between these two types.

Because Ne is dominant for ENTPs, they tend to be more talkative, assertive, and demonstrative in their presentation. They also tend to have broader interests than INTPs. To illustrate the breadth of their interests, consider the life of an ENTP friend of mine. He owns his own media company, supports a large family, is actively involved in reviving local arts and culture, owns a boat for weekend fun, plays a couple different instruments, dabbles in painting and beer brewing, and also finds time for running and kayaking. He is always experimenting with something new. Those seeking a historical example might consider the life of ENTP Benjamin Franklin, whose interests and vocations were even more extensive and more diverse than those of my friend.

While INTPs may enjoy a few different hobbies, they typically don't have the physical energy to sustain the frenetic lifestyle common to ENTPs. INTPs tend to invest the lion's share of their time and energy in one or two interest areas, which are often more solitary in nature. INTPs are also more likely to identify themselves primarily as intellectuals, whereas ENTPs may be reluctant to narrow their identity in such a way.

Generally speaking, ENTPs display less patience for writing, but tend to be better orators than INTPs. Because of their extraversion, ENTPs are also more at home in leadership positions.

ENTPs also have a "fun loving" streak that can be absent in INTPs. As dominant Perceivers, they love to laugh and play games. I once administered a values inventory and was a bit surprised when a couple ENTPs marked "having fun" as one of their top priorities. ENTPs are more genuinely easygoing than INTPs. While INTPs may appear easygoing in the company of strangers, those who know them realize they are more focused and agenda-driven (Ti), as well as less spontaneous, than they may outwardly appear.

Philosophically, INTPs and ENTPs typically think along similar lines. In many cases, their differences can be attributed to their respective inferior functions. For example, ENTPs' inferior Si may compel them to latch onto certain traditions or periods of history that they find personally meaningful. I know several ENTPs, for instance, who feel strongly connected to the history and traditions of their religious faith. Studying related rituals, archaeology, artifacts, culture, and geography seems deeply meaningful to them, since these things ostensibly serve to marry their Ne (religious ideas/ concepts) and Si (the physical/ historical embodiment of those ideas). Granted, some ENTPs (e.g., Benjamin Franklin, Walt Disney) may opt to marry N and S in alternative ways, such as through invention, innovation, or various artistic enterprises.

INTPs, by contrast, are more concerned with marrying Ti and Fe, making Si historical traditions and artifacts less important than the pursuit of essential truths. INTPs are more willing to shed what they see as dispensable historical or cultural elements in order to extract what they see as the essential concepts and ideas. For example, INTPs may see the historical facts of Jesus's life as far less important than the ideas he espoused, while ENTPs may be enamored with the history, culture, and details of his life.

INTP vs. ISTP

INTPs also share much in common with ISTPs. In sharing the same dominant and inferior function, these types struggle with many of the same inferior function issues. Where they differ, of course, is in the middle portion of their functional stack—their auxiliary and tertiary functions.

ISTPs use Extraverted Sensing (Se) as their auxiliary function. While Si is conservative with respect to sensations and the material world, Se is more materially liberal and novelty-oriented (although this may be somewhat attenuated in ISTPs due to their dominant Ti). Consequently, ISTPs often have broader tastes and stronger interests in food, sex, and physical activities than INTPs.

Se is also more "hands on" and concrete than Si. This makes ISTPs more inclined toward physical activity in general, and hands-on work in particular. ISTPs are less opposed to hard physical labor or "getting their hands dirty" than INTPs tend to be. They often enjoy hands-on technical work, functioning as surgeons, pilots, mechanics, and the like. They also make excellent craftsmen, using their Se to attend to the finest physical details. While INTPs are ideationally creative, ISTPs are mechanically and kinesthetically creative.

Se attunes to the concrete details and sensory information of the environment by way of the five senses. This compels ISTPs to scan the environment for interesting sensory novelties, allowing them to notice details that other types might miss. ISTPs may utilize this attention to external detail in any number of ways. One of my ISTP friends, for instance, enjoys scavenging nearby fields for arrowheads. As he saunters about, he scans the environment in hopes of finding another lost treasure. After locating an arrowhead, he further enlists his Se to explore its shape, texture, and other features.

Se also differs from Ne in that it is not an abstract function. So while INTPs enjoy sitting back and discussing ideas, ISTPs would often prefer to be "doing" something. Even watching sports or movies can be more stimulating to ISTPs than conversation, since it stimulates their Se and allows them to vicariously participate in the action.

When it comes to worldview, ISTPs tend to be more conventional and traditional than INTPs. This is especially true of ISTPs raised in traditional-minded households or communities. ISTPs' tendency toward conventionality stems from the fact that their Se is less ideationally open than INTPs' Ne.

In short, INTPs and ISTPs are primarily distinguished by the differing interests and propensities of their respective auxiliary functions. For this reason, ITPs who have failed to adequately exercise and develop their auxiliary function may struggle to discern their status as an INTP versus an ISTP.

INTP vs. INFP

Since this type comparison involves T-F differences, gender may play a confounding role. I have found that INTP and INFP males are often strikingly similar in many ways. Both are ruggedly individualistic and deeply concerned with protecting their personal autonomy and freedom. They even display similar body types, tending toward ectomorphy (i.e., long and lean) combined with mild mesomorphy (i.e., lightly muscled). They may also dress fairly similarly, prioritizing comfort and minimalism (although INFPs may be a bit more grunge or hipster). Both may buck conventions when it comes to personal care and grooming, although this can vary widely by social context.

INTPs and INFPs may also opt for similar living conditions, typically along minimalist, Bohemian lines. Both like the idea of living lightly, granting them the freedom to pick up and relocate at the drop of a hat. Both tend to downplay the importance of bourgeois comforts, fearing that too much comfort might beget boredom and apathy. To cultivate an intense and meaningful life, both types are willing to forgo Se comforts in favor of more time doing what they love.

INTPs and INFPs are also prone to adopting a rather romantic view of nature and primitive living, inspired, at least in part, by their distaste for conventional work. Of the two, however, INFPs are more likely to actually take to the woods. It's rare to meet an INFP male with no interest in hiking or the outdoors. It is not at all uncommon for them to escape to nature for weeks, even months, on end. While INTPs' Ne-Si duo may inspire some degree of interest in nature or hiking, INFPs' Fi-Ne-Si trio confers a deeper and more authentic love of the outdoors.

Presumably due to their inferior Fe, INTPs can seem a bit more reliant on other people than INFPs, even if merely for background noise. Whether they are willing to admit it or not, INTPs are afraid of being isolated and cut-off from people. Similarly, because of their inferior Te, INFPs may harbor fears of being cut-off from the Te system.

INFPs and INTPs also share interests and preferences that we can ascribe to the Ne-Si function pair. Academically, for instance, both types might take interest in biology and environmental studies, stemming from their Ne-Si interest in the natural world. INFPs, however, seem more apt to actually become biologists or environmental scientists, due to their dominant Fi, as well as their Te love of science. Their Fi-Te combo also disposes them to take interest in fiction and science fiction, whereas INTPs are more inclined toward non-fiction.

INTPs and INFPs are also alike in their indecisiveness. Both are constantly making new plans, which is their way of trying to impose order on their lives. More often than not, however, they end up diverging from, or even jettisoning, their plans, in favor of a promising alternative. This can be attributed to their shared Ne, which produces an abundance of new ideas, but is also notorious for questioning the ideas it just produced. Other types may find it humorous how often INPs seem to have a new grand plan for their lives.

As F dominants, INFPs are more authentically inclined toward the arts, culture, and music than INTPs. INTPs, by contrast, are most engaged when researching, philosophizing, discussing ideas with others, or working on their personal projects. INFPs also display more F tendencies with respect to caring for animals, plants, the needy, or those with special needs. Although INTP females may be more nurturing and interested in children than INTP males, INFP females display particularly strong interests in children. Most want their own children and see childrearing as one of their primary aims in life. INFPs are also more apt to take up cooking or gardening than INTPs.

INFPs are less likely than INTPs to struggle with thoughts and fears about meaninglessness. As F dominants, a sense of meaning and value is readily accessible to INFPs. Instead of meaning-related concerns, INFPs may worry that life or the world will somehow prove irrational or nonsensical (Te). This is why so many INFPs end up studying math, science, computers, etc. Through such pursuits, they, wittingly or not, strive to make sense of and bring greater order to the world. Similarly, INTPs, wisely or not, may turn to human studies as a way of better understanding humanity and the human condition (Fe).

INTP vs. INTJ

Despite having no functions in common, INTPs and INTJs have notable similarities. Both are deeply skeptical, philosophical, and penetrating in their thinking. Since both types seek an accurate understanding of themselves and the world, they can enjoy extended discussions and find common ground on a number of topics. But they also differ in some important ways. At times, however, these differences can seem subtle and require careful analysis to understand their origin.

Outwardly distinguishing INTJs from INTPs can often be fairly easy. Since INTJs extravert Thinking (Te), an outsider quickly encounters their rational nature. They are measured, articulate, and direct, even blunt, in their presentation. They see themselves as strong debaters and are undeterred in challenging those making dubious assertions about truth. It pains them to let spurious statements go unchallenged.

INTPs, by contrast, extravert Intuition (Ne) and Feeling (Fe). And assuming the INTP is not overly awkward or anxious, these functions allow him or her to blend more easily into social situations. Moreover, because their Fe is inferior, INTPs are generally less comfortable directly challenging others' assertions. They are more selective in asserting their views and in displaying their rational side. They are disposed to posing questions or positing possibilities (Ne) rather than making strong assertions (Fe). Because Ne is more divergent and dithering than Ni, INTPs also tend to experience and display less conviction about things than INTJs do.

Since their Ni and Te work convergently, INTJs are rightly understood as systematizers. Te strives to see the world's systems and operations be controlled, orderly, and rational. It pushes for a standardized set of collective methods for evaluating and implementing what is rational. This is why INTJs are often champions of science and the scientific method. Their Te is more positivistic and forward-moving than INTPs' Ti. Once their Ni vision is clear, INTJs use Te to formulate definitions, classifications, plans, or procedures.

While INTPs may find a fair amount of philosophical resonance with INTJs, they are averse to certain Te propensities. Namely, when INTJs propose external formalizing and structuring, INTPs tend to resist it. In lieu of making external systems more rational, Ti orients INTPs' rationality toward themselves and their own ideas. INTPs are largely concerned with ensuring that their own lives, worldview, and personal philosophy are rational. Their aversion to Te methods also explains why INTPs can be less enthusiastic toward science and its methods.

INTJs make excellent troubleshooters, consultants, analysts, mathematicians, physicians, and scientists. INTPs differ from INTJs in this respect. INTPs can readily generate ideas or possible ways of addressing a problem, but seem less capable of forming firm conclusions about what is happening or what should be done. If someone wants a firm opinion or direct advice about resolving a complex issue, they are far more likely to get it from an INTJ than an INTP.

Despite their knack for problem solving, INTJs may struggle to find their niche in the world because of their strong idealism. Many INTJs don't just want to solve any problem, but to identify and address the world's most pressing issues. This is not always a bad thing. If there is a personality type that can see the big picture and zero-in on its key issues, it is probably the INTJ. An INTJ friend of mine is always talking about "leverage points." His goal is to identify key leverage points, issues he feels are the most foundational to the world's problems. Once INTJs discern what they see as key insights or leverage points, they may, at least for a time, function as advocates, activists, or reformers (this is why some INTJs test as Enneagram Ones). They may continue in such a role until they encounter what they see as insurmountable resistance or until they discover a better way to effect change.

Since their Ti is directed inwardly, INTPs tend to be more interested in understanding themselves and their pet interests than directly changing the world. As is true for many INFPs, the self—its, nature, health, and identity—is a constant reference point for INTPs. This may shed light on the origin of the notion that INTPs are interested in "knowledge for its own sake." Since INTPs apply their knowledge inwardly (Ti), others are blinded to the process and may therefore consider them mere "idea hedonists." But the fact is that INTPs do apply their knowledge. They apply it to their quest for self-betterment and optimal living. Thus, the notion that INTPs are leisurely and aimlessly consuming ideas for mere pleasure misses the mark. In fact, this would probably be truer of INTJs, who, because of their Ni dominance, are predominantly Perceivers.

While INTJs may also display an interest in self-knowledge because of their introversion and their tertiary Fi, it is often to a lesser degree than is typical of INTPs. Since Te comes before Fi in their functional stack, INTJs are, wittingly or not, generally willing to sacrifice some degree of self-understanding (Fi) for the sake of their rational pursuits (Te).

With these things in mind, we can see how INTJs and INTPs work in different directions. INTJs focus more directly on external systems (Te) and, in the process, come to better understand themselves (Fi). INTPs, by contrast, focus first on understanding and regulating themselves (Ti) and then seek to express that understanding in creative ways (Ne). This is not to say that INTPs merely ignore what is happening in the outside world (although they may be less concerned with it than INTJs are). Rather, they analyze it with an eye toward furthering their understanding of themselves (Ti) and the human condition (Fe). Because INTPs have Fe rather than Te in their functional stack, they are drawn to exploring Fe sorts of information. This is why they share much in common with INFJs (who also use Fe and Ti) and tend to be most captivated by things like philosophy, psychology, and religion. The T information INTPs do manage to collect (e.g., scientific or historical facts) is often done with hopes of furthering their understanding of themselves and human nature.

While INTJs excel in careers involving real-world evaluation and problem solving, INTPs will often gravitate toward more divergent or expressive sorts of work. They enjoy using their Ne to make broad connections among ideas, an endeavor they find deeply interesting and meaningful. Again, their goal is not necessarily to solve the world's problems (although this might occur indirectly), but to clarify concepts and conceptual relationships in a way that is personally applicable or meaningful. This too may contribute to their "idea-hedonist" reputation.

Because of their Fi, INTJs also seem more prone to emphasize the uniqueness of individuals (including themselves) than INTPs are.

Like other Fi types, some INTJs are quick to dismiss typology, at least in part, because it is perceived as offensive to their convictions about individual uniqueness. Fi may also dispose them to latch onto certain negative childhood experiences. They may spend significant time trying to analyze their childhood in order to discern how their circumstances impacted who they are as individuals. In such INTJs, one can often trace a connection between their Fi sentiments and their Ni-Te objectives. In many cases, the things that most disturb their Fi sense of justice are the things they hope to understand and remedy via Ni-Te. In other words, such INTJs are motivated not only by perceived shortcomings in external systems (Te), but also by their own negative experiences (Fi). The degree to which Fi plays a role in a given INTJ's concerns and interests might largely explain whether he scores as an Enneagram 5w6 (lower Fi involvement) or 5w4 (higher Fi involvement).

INTPs, by contrast, generally focus less on negative feelings or past experiences. They are less likely to hold grudges or attribute causality to childhood circumstances. This might be understood as a Ti-Fi difference.

10. CLOSING THOUGHTS

Life as an INTP is not without its challenges. It may take years, even decades, for INTPs to clarify their identity and desired vocation. It is relatively rare that they find an easy or immediate fit into an existing career field. Part of the problem is their disdain for authority. They are naturally averse to rules (save those they make for themselves) and resistant to taking orders from others.

Not only are INTPs the most independent personality type, but also one of the most restless. They are constantly searching and experimenting, while simultaneously dodging and resisting external obligations to ensure adequate time and space to themselves.

INTPs are seekers of both truth and meaning. From a typological standpoint, they are seeking their inferior F, which represents a sort of holy grail of meaning and value for Thinking-dominant types. Indeed, INTPs can be terrified at the prospect of meaninglessness, since without a sense of F meaning, all of their T endeavors can seem empty and futile. Paradoxically, however, it is largely through consistent use and development of their T that INTPs cultivate a meaningful life. This again is why their work can seem so important, providing a context for employing their T and experiencing the F rewards of doing so.

Although INTPs may claim to be interested in finding hard or absolute truth, we should not always take this claim at face value. After all, if

INTPs were to finally discover whatever it is they are looking for, they would soon become bored and start searching for new questions to explore. So what INTPs are actually seeking may be right under their nose—the process of seeking itself. This is not to say they will never draw some conclusions or feel they are making progress, but only that what is most important is that there always be more questions awaiting them. They want to explore questions that are interesting, meaningful, and somewhat open-ended. They want enough truth to feel convinced they are somehow getting at the reality of things, but not so much where matters seem too easy or clear-cut.

In light of the above, we should also consider whether INTPs' fear of meaninglessness might be a fear of lacking new or interesting questions to explore. Put differently, INTPs may be afraid of finding answers to or losing interest in what they see as life's most meaningful questions. If, for instance, they were to finally discover "how to live," would they still find life interesting and worth living?

It is here we encounter a difference between Phase II and Phase III of development, as well as the difficulty and resistance associated with the transition. In Phase II, INTPs are literally addicted to asking questions and seeking answers. This may be fueled, at least in part, by their desire to advance in their careers and secure anticipated ego rewards. Hence, from the vantage point of Phase II, Phase III may seem rather mundane, since it entails a reduction of the intensity and adrenaline associated with ego-related pursuits. Phase II INTPs may find it difficult to see how happiness is possible without the continued pursuit of intense highs.

INTPs who do manage to make the transition to Phase III experience a deeper sense of peace, wholeness, and satisfaction. With diminished tension and disparity between their Ti and Fe, they find it easier to enjoy a broader swath of life, including their relationships, with less urgency and anxiety. With the ego-centered rollercoaster of Phase II behind them, they devote less time and energy to feverish striving and more to savoring and being present in each new moment.

ADDITIONAL RESOURCES

For more information on INTPs' personality, careers, relationships, etc., I encourage you to visit my website:

PersonalityJunkie.com

You may also wish to explore my other books:

The INTP Quest: INTPs' Search for their Core Self, Purpose, & Philosophy

The 16 Personality Types: Profiles, Theory, & Type Development

My True Type: Clarifying Your Personality Type, Preferences & Functions

Best to you!

A.J. Drenth

Made in the USA
Coppell, TX
08 August 2021

60149264R10090